The Executive's
New Computer

Six Keys to Systems Success

OLIVER WIGHT

The Executive's
New Computer

Six Keys to Systems Success

RESTON PUBLISHING COMPANY, INC., *Reston, Virginia*

© 1972 by
RESTON PUBLISHING COMPANY, INC.
Reston, Virginia.

10 9 8 7 6 5 4 3 2

ISBN: 0-87909-247-5

Library of Congress Catalog Card Number: 76-171477
Printed in the United States of America

This book is dedicated to a proposition:

Systems are tools for the manager,
not toys for the technician

. . .and it is about time we dispensed with all
the pious nonsense about computer systems and
got down to **business.**

Foreword

This is not a book of business humor. It is intended as straight-forward, practical advice to people who want to use computers more successfully. I have, however, tried to "hold the mirror to folly" in some sections. Until businessmen really understand the hypocrisy, mock-heroics, and the naive pursuit of sophistication that have characterized the early years of the computer age I question that they will be able to see computer systems in a real business perspective.

Some of the consultants, college professors, and data processing/systems people are reluctant to face up to the lack of success in computer applications. In practice they continue to defend and promote the same approaches that have resulted in failure in the past. Many seem to believe that it serves the cause of "sophistication" to adopt a posture of professional hypocrisy. I personally believe that we badly need a more businesslike attitude toward computer systems and that the cause of progress is not served by situations like these:

1. Some computer manufacturers offer programs that can be used to implement production and inventory control systems. Most do not yet use these programs in their own manufacturing facilities! One of them offers a program that was developed in 1964 at one of their own plants. While they have used this program as a marketing tool for years, it has never been[1] successfully implemented by any customer and is not really considered successful by their plant people, even though they regularly give plant tours "explaining" it.

2. A consultant, who confesses privately that most systems fail because management does not take a realistic attitude toward systems, publicizes a new computer application program he is promoting as follows: " . . .it will take complete charge of the planning, scheduling, and control of the inventory and production process in a job shop. It is truly remarkable in the manner in which it performs this function, eliminating the need for the human decision wherever possible. . . ." In my opinion, this is Madison Avenue-type nonsense. It only serves to perpetuate the misconception that systems will run businesses. *"Complete charge—FANTASTIC!"*[2]

3. A college professor teaches a course about Management Information Systems (MIS). He conveys the impression to his students that most companies have one. He indicates that a "total management commitment and a financial investment of up to seven million dollars will be required

---

*[1] I last checked this in early 1970. The source was a company executive responsible for marketing application programs.

*[2] *FANTASTIC* is a word that is currently being taught in finishing schools to be used instead of the word "Bullshit." "Bullshit" is a unique word for which there is no real synonym. Anyone working in the areas of computers, systems, and consulting who does not feel the urge to use this word frequently is probably becoming brainwashed.

to achieve an MIS." In private, he confides that he has never really seen an MIS!

4. An auditing firm that has some serious misconceptions about basic inventory management approaches has, in five tries (that I know of), been unable to install successfully the type of system they recommend. They not only continue to prosper, but none of these auditing clients that have used their management consulting services unsuccessfully seem to have been dissatisfied enough to discontinue use of their auditing services!

5. A corporate data processing and systems man (Manager of MIS) has a department with a seven-figure annual budget. His company has few systems that have produced any tangible results. He, personally, has designed and installed them all ("the users are not sophisticated enough to understand") and blames the lack of systems success on "management's failure to enforce discipline."

His main effort now, in response to recent management criticism about the cost of his operation, is to replace much of his equipment with lower-rental equipment of many brands. This not only gives the impression that he is responding to management pressures, it also casts him in the role of "thinking man" (not locked into one or two vendors!) among his peers. He assumes the posture of being a data processing "professional." He is quite proud of his company's computer "progress." He is quick to boast about their on line terminals and other technical sophistication. He describes himself as being "in the data processing mainstream."

This is the world of hypocrisy, "technological exhibitionism,"[3] and the mystique of the computer and its high priests that exists today. But I am encouraged by the response that data processing people, systems people, and college professors have had to talks I have given discussing these problems. Many of them are fed up with all the baloney they read and hear and want to make a

---

*[3] Mumford, Lewis; *The Pentagon of Power*, Harcourt, Brace, Jovanovich, 1970

more significant contribution to business success. They are becoming more interested in results than the false goddess of sophistication.

The folly of sophistication as an end in itself is one of the major themes of this book. The notion that the development of "Totally Integrated Management Information Systems" should be a primary goal for many companies, for example, is absurd. It is also foolish to assume that the best solution to most companies' problems is to "design a simulation model of the business." One of the classical misdirections of the early years of the computer age was over-sophistication. We have learned — the hard way — that scientific management has not usually been the real payoff application. Most of the payoffs today are in the areas of "massive manipulation of data." And the most successful systems are the ones that are designed to support — not supplant — the activities of people.

This may sound distastefully unsophisticated to some systems, O.R., and computer people. It is the thrust of this book. Hopefully, even those people who believe that computer systems *will* really run businesses without human intervention someday should be able to appreciate the approach of "walk before you run." We never would have made the moon if the Wright brothers had not been willing to settle for something less.

The purpose of this book is to distill the knowledge gained from observing many failures and the rare successes in the still early years of computer application and to pass it on. The *six keys to systems success* are developed in Chapter I. The subsequent chapters deal with each key in more detail. They are summarized in checklist number one.

In this day of the instant authority and self-appointed expert, any reader deserves to know his author's background. I worked for the Raybestos Division of Raybestos-Manhattan for nine years in all phases of production and inventory control. This was followed by three and one-half years as a corporate production control consultant to the thirteen divisions of the Stanley Works. Between

February, 1965 and February, 1968 I was with the Manufacturing Industries Marketing Department of IBM. My job as Industry Education Manager gave me a chance to visit many companies and talk with thousands of executives and professionals about computer applications. Since then, as president of my own company and a partner in Plossl and Wight Associates, I have visited and worked with many manufacturing companies as a consultant. I am co-author of the best-selling technical book, *"Production and Inventory Control."*[4] Discussions with about 2000 attendees each year at courses and talks I have given on this subject have added insights into the problems of installing effective computer systems.

Several books on computer systems are available today, and several people have encouraged me to write one more book aimed at the general market. They have pointed out that by using manufacturing control examples I may not reach the hospital administrator, insurance executive, and others who are frustrated with *their* computers. I have talked with people from several of these fields who have agreed that my "six keys" are valid outside of manufacturing control. But it would be out of character, in a book that ridicules hypocrisy, to pose as a general "computer systems expert" — whatever that is supposed to be!

Examples from the field of Inventory and Production Management have accordingly been used. Partly, of course, because this is the area I know best. But, more importantly, these examples are helpful in illustrating advice that could easily sound like "motherhood." Of course, this field is also the one with the biggest payoff potential in most manufacturing companies.

Chapters 1, 2, and 7 of this book deal primarily with philosophy. I hope you will give them the same serious consideration you give to the practical advice of Chapters 3, 4, 5, and 6. Without a valid philosophy of business management, there can be no consistent application of principles and techniques. Several check lists are included at the back of the book for the manager

---

[4] Englewood Cliffs, New Jersey: Prentice-Hall, Inc., 1967.

who would like a distillation of some of the ideas that can be used on a day-to-day basis.

Acknowledgments to all the people who have helped and contributed to my knowledge would fill a book in themselves. Dick Alban, George Brandenburg, Jim Burlingame, Dave Garwood, Walt Goddard, Al Janesky, Joe Orlicky, Jerry Pisani, George Plossl, Paul Rosa, and Bill Wassweiler deserve special mention for their contributions to my knowledge of this subject. Obviously, the opinions expressed in this book are strictly my own — my friends should suffer no onus because of my convictions.

I would also like to thank my secretary, Terry Peterson, whose good humor helped to make the work go fast. Lastly, I would like, in a few feeble words, to acknowledge the constant help and encouragement my wife and business associate, Betty, has contributed. Other husbands who know how much a wife can help in so many ways will really understand how weak these words are in expressing my appreciation.

The Executive

There is a famous Hans Christian Andersen story entitled "The Emperor's New Clothes." This is the story of an emperor who was particularly vain and fond of his dress. One day, two swindlers came to town and told him they knew how to weave the most beautiful fabrics imaginable. They said the colors and patterns were not only unusually fine, but that the clothes were made of a cloth that had the peculiar quality of becoming invisible to any person who was not fit for the office he held or who was impossibly dull. At great expense, they made these "clothes" for the emperor and, of course, nobody wanted to admit that they could not see the cloth. When the clothes were finally completed, the emperor walked through the public streets in a procession to show them off. Everybody cheered and clapped except for one little child who said, "But he has nothing on."

There are many parallels between this story and the application of computers to business. Let me tell you a little bit about an Executive and his New Computer.

Back in 1959, Lionel Lambert, who was just about to become the vice-president of a medium-sized company, attended a technical conference where he heard a great deal about the computer. He decided that his company needed a computer so that they could have a Management Information System. When his computer came in, they immediately put the payroll on it and eliminated two clerks. They then looked around to see where else they could start to build a Management Information System, and they looked at inventory control. The computer systems man went to the inventory control man and said, "The computer age has arrived. We are now going to help you by putting your system on the computer." The inventory control man said, "I've got enough problems. Can't you go help someone else?" Nevertheless, the systems man persisted with top management backing and, after much effort, they finally succeeded in mechanizing the Kardex records with the result that they got rid of two more clerks. But, of course, in the meantime they had added several systems people, a couple of programmers, and a good many keypunch operators in addition to the computer itself.

Lionel Lambert found that he was achieving a degree of fame at his country club. All the other executives were asking him about computers, and he explained the problems and benefits of computerizing. Something deep inside him told him that things were not going as well as he had hoped, but every time his spirits sagged, another group of visitors would be brought through the company by the computer salesman to be shown the wonders of computerization. While Lionel could not say very much about real, tangible results (like profits, for example), he always explained the great benefits that they were looking forward to in the future. He began to be called on to give talks on developing a Management Information System and even had his picture on a magazine cover as one of the pioneers of computerization in industry.

By this time, Lionel was deeply engrossed in installing his second generation computer. This would enable him to get *daily* inventory reports, rather than weekly inventory reports, from his mechanized Kardex system. It would also enable him to put in some Scientific Inventory Control techniques. After a year of trial and tribulation, the new computer went on the air. There were still no real tangible results in controlling inventories and the people in the inventory control department were extremely unhappy with the system because they did not understand all the fancy mathematics, and they were frustrated with the inaccurate data. A few of them were even heard to whisper that they would sure like to get back to the good old days of the Kardex.

Meanwhile, Lionel decided to bring in a consultant to help them install a system called "Stochastic Rescheduling." This technique was designed to reschedule the entire plant daily and to generate a priority dispatch list for the foremen. Again, people flocked to Lionel's plant to see this new system which was highly touted in magazine articles, by the computer salesman, and by the consulting firm that helped to put the system in. The only problem with this system was that the foremen apparently did not operate by the dispatch list. On a trip through the plant, Lionel found the foremen working to hand written "hot lists" that were passed down from the assembly departments to the sub-assembly department, etc. He got his foremen together and told them that they had to work to the new computerized dispatch list. The group of foremen convinced him that if they did, he would not be able to meet his monthly shipping budget because they would not be making the parts that were *really* needed!

This disturbed Lionel. As he reflected on his computer investment, he decided that he really needed to know more about managing the computer effort. So he went off to a computer school where he learned Binary, Octal, Hexadecimal and lots of other good things. He came back with a warm feeling about computers, as if he really understood them, but the more he thought about his computer problems, the more he wound up talking to himself, often in Hexadecimal, "FF-FF-FF!"

By this time, Lionel had ordered his third generation

computer. The order was placed rather hurriedly because it came as a shock to him one day when he went to the country club to find out that many other companies had already ordered their third generation computers and that his company, instead of being a leader, seemed to be slipping behind.

One night, after the computer had been installed, Lionel sat working very late at his desk. As he reviewed his increasing computer expense he found it difficult to tell himself honestly that the tangible results really justified the effort and expense. His fame in business circles and the popularity of his talks on "Achieving an MIS," "Anatomy of a Data Base," did give him some reassurance that he must be headed in the right direction. Just then, he spied a very interesting letter in his mail basket. He picked it out and started to open it when Madeline, the cleaning woman, stuck her head in the door. "I see you're working late, Mr. Lambert." "That's right," said Lionel. "These are busy days." "I wonder if I could ask you a question," said Madeline. "I'm a stockholder and I note that our earnings per share have been going down over the last few years. Does it have anything to do with that computer installation that seems to get bigger and bigger all the time? I notice that we've got more systems people, more programmers, and more equipment every time we turn around." Lionel flushed a little. "Well, hardly, Madeline. You see, what we are really up against is the profit squeeze. If you look at other companies in business, you will see that most of them are in a profit squeeze also." "That may be true, Mr. Lambert," said Madeline. "But I understand from some of my friends that most of the other companies have computers. . . . "

This thought disturbed Lionel. As he pondered he went back to reading his mail. The interesting letter he had spied turned out to be from an executive search company. It said,

"Your Nationally Renowned Reputation As An Executive Who Has Successfully Installed Management Information Systems Makes You Particularly Attractive To

Our Client. We Are Willing To Offer You $10,000 Per Year More Than You Are Currently Making If You Will Come On As Vice-President In Charge Of Information Systems."

Lionel thought about this for a while and thought about what his experiences had taught him. He decided to take the offer.

Contents

Contents

The Executive's New Computer

Six Keys to Systems Success

1

Why Computer Systems Usually Fail

"Never before in the history of human endeavor have so many invested so much to so little avail."

THE UNFULFILLED PROMISE

The stored-program, electronic digital computer really began to gain acceptance in business in the late 1950's. By the mid-1960's many companies had computers installed. But success seemed elusive. Today most businessmen who read or talk to others in similar positions are increasingly aware of the fact that most computers simply have not paid off — in spite of the fact that practically every company of any size uses one or more.[1]

The failure of computers to come anywhere near attaining

---

[1] This statement, like most others in this book, is based on my knowledge of computer applications in manufacturing companies.

their real potential is no secret, but, even today, most executives don't realize how bad the situation really is. The average person is exposed primarily to "gee whiz" magazine articles on the wonders of computerization, being constantly bombarded by literature advertising new hardware and programs, and constantly hearing rather vague tales of success in other companies. His experience is limited to one — or at best a few — companies and it is easy for him to believe that he and a small minority of other businessmen are suffering frustration, while a large number of others have really attained a great deal of success.

This simply is not true. It's the old shell game — there's always somebody down the street or over in the next town who's "really doing a great job" with computers. The *truth* is that the number of companies actually getting a payoff from computers represents a very, very small percentage of the total that have tried.

What is success?

Success Must Be Judged By Business — Not Computer — Standards

A successful company is one that is able to give either better customer service, or better quality, or increase their volume, or reduce their inventory, etc., because of their computer service. The prime measure of success is a very simple one! *Are they operating better than they were before they had a computer?* By any *business* standard, does their computer investment return them as much as it has cost them, or has it simply been an expensive learning process.

In most companies the picture is muddled. If you asked these questions directly, you'd get conflicting answers from different people. There is always someone — usually with some proprietary interest in the computer system — who claims that the company could not be operating today without it. To a great extent this is "poppy-cock." Manufacturing companies built locomotives back in the 1800's and did it without computers. Not that it cannot be done more efficiently with computers today, but to assume that a complex business cannot possibly be run without a computer is to ignore the facts of history.

On the other hand, many complex businesses *can* be run far more effectively with computer systems. This is an old "pitch" of the computer salesman, but today there are a few companies that are really making it happen. They *do* run more efficiently using computer systems. Others have not gotten really involved with computer systems yet. But because the potential application is so obvious the vast majority of companies today *do* have computers, but they are not getting dramatic operational results. *Unlike the company that is getting results, or even the company that has no significant computer investment as yet, they are paying the bill but not getting the payoff.* The worst of both worlds!

SIX TESTED WAYS TO FAIL

There are a limited number of reasons for systems failure. As in any other type of analysis it is important to segregate the "vital few from the trivial many." The vital few reasons for systems failure are:

1. SYSTEM TOO SOPHISTICATED AND AMBITIOUS.
2. APPLICATION NOT SOUND.
3. SYSTEMS PEOPLE ASSUMED — AND MANAGEMENT ABDICATED — RESPONSIBILITY FOR SYSTEM DE-SIGN.
4. DESIGNED TO SUPPLANT — NOT SUPPORT — THE USER.
5. OPTIMISTIC IMPLEMENTATION.
6. COMPANY INCAPABLE OF MANAGING WITH A SYSTEM.

Chart 1, *Six Key Reasons for Systems Failure*, shows a list of eight companies picked from many where systems have not been successful. The reasons for systems failure are also shown on the

CHART 1.   SIX KEY REASONS FOR SYSTEMS FAILURE

Company A	– Reasons No. 1 and No. 3	– Too ambitious and sophisticated, designed by systems people.
Company B	– Reasons No. 2, No. 3 and No. 5	– Good technique improperly applied, designed by systems people, optimistic implementation.
Company C	– Reason No. 3	– Systems people chose the computer applications and designed the systems.
Company D	– Reasons No. 3 and No. 6.	– Unable to manage with a system, management abdicated responsibility.
Company E	– Reason No. 6	– Unable to manage with a system.
Company F	– Reasons No. 2 and No. 3	– Wrong application, designed by systems people.
Company G	– Reason No. 6	– Unable to manage with a system.
Company H	– Reasons No. 1, No. 3 and No. 4	– Too sophisticated, designed by systems people, designed to supplant the user.

chart. The numbers refer to the reasons listed above. Company A, for example, failed for reasons 1 and 3 above.

Let's take a look at each of these companies briefly. Company A is a very large company with very progressive management and many plants located throughout the United States. They wanted to develop an overall manufacturing control system that would tie all plants together. This system was going to involve a huge computer investment, teleprocessing, and a great deal of "on-line" application. Originally budgeted for $40,000,000, the costs went well over $100,000,000 — with no end in sight — before the effort was abandoned. The plant people were *theoretically* involved, but *actually* not involved, and practically all of the systems design work was being done by systems people. The system became highly sophisticated and collapsed of its own weight before it ever got off the ground.

Company B makes an assembled product and had been profitable for many years, until a consultant was brought in to install an inventory control system. The man who was sent in was far more knowledgable about computers than he was about manufacturing, and, in fact, he had a high disdain for manufacturing people in general and foremen in particular. His lack of knowledge about production and inventory control was not a disadvantage at all in his eyes. Since he did not know much, he had no idea how much he did not know!

His system was a total disaster. It was the wrong type of inventory system for this company's product. It was installed with the "cold turkey" approach (the new system was installed all at once). The plant immediately shut down and it was a number of weeks later before the combined efforts of the company people — particularly the foremen — were able to get it operating again. This systems man had chosen an improper application, management had given him the major responsibility for systems design, and, while management thought that the users were involved, the users were completely confident that a major consulting firm couldn't possibly install a system that would be anything but successful. Because of this misconception, management paid very little attention to the progress or nature of the systems work. Company B is certainly one of the worst systems failures of all time. Even though they have managed to stay in business, they have been unable to reach their previous high-profit levels — for a number of reasons. Among these certainly is the contribution of a confusing, improperly designed, and poorly implemented computer system.

Company C is a large aerospace-electronics oriented manufacturer. They have a Director of Management Information Systems who reports right to the president. The only time this man gets any users involved is when he's justifying a new piece of hardware. Once he's got it, his interest lies primarily in doing things that will impress his data processing peers rather than contribute to company profits. He is quick to boast about his "on-line, real time teleprocessing in multiprogramming mode." When I talked with the manufacturing vice president of his company to find out what *he* was getting from this elegant computer system, he was brief but eloquent. He said, *"Paper — mountains of useless, confusing paper!"*

Company D is a conservative old-line company where the management people have always been skeptical of systems and would go to any lengths to avoid doing almost anything systematically. They have a few reasonably successful systems, but their attempt to put in a shop-floor control system was a dismal failure for the following reasons:

1. The production control manager, in spite of giving a great deal of lip service to the system, really took the attitude "let's see if these systems guys can really pull this one off." He expected the system to run the shop and kept his people totally aloof from it. This probably was the major reason why the system failed, but it's important to consider also. . . .

2. Very little in the way of systematic management has been achieved in this company over the years. Most of their old-line manufacturing people look on systems as "sissy stuff" and feel that it is considerably more manly to do *fire fighting* than *fire prevention.* They will tell anyone that their problems are unique and unsolvable because they have a "job shop." They have had considerable trouble making a profit in recent years. They attribute this to outside factors beyond their control.

Company E manufactures an assembled product. They installed a new inventory system involving material requirements planning. This technique (described more fully in Chapter 3) is a means of converting assembly requirements into sub-assembly and parts requirements by "exploding" bills of material via computer. Company E did *almost* everything properly. Their application was sound, their users got involved, their system was not overly sophisticated, and they implemented the system very, very carefully. Unfortunately, this system, although still operating today, cannot be considered successful by the standards discussed above. When this system was installed the company was preparing for a strike, introducing a new product, and closing an old plant. They introduced into their requirements plan a schedule that called for *five times* more machines than they had ever produced before! The computer, of course, ordered these parts, and, not surprisingly, their assembly production rate did not increase very much at all. (For one thing, when a computer system generates a huge parts shortage list, the system is no longer really operative. Nobody can expedite all of the parts at once, and they must revert to a manual system to find out what parts are *really* needed, *today*.) Inventory increased, skeptical members of middle management and the production and inventory control department realized that things really weren't any different (because their prime reliance was on their manual shortage lists), and the system never really got off the ground. In this company there is a general management philosophy of operating in "crisis mode."

Company F installed a shop-floor control system long before they had an effective inventory system to plan what items they really needed. This is not an uncommon occurrence and falls under the general category of a *massive assault on the symptoms.* This system, however, was strongly backed by the manufacturing vice president, and he insisted that the foremen work to it. Before that, the foremen, through communication with production control people, "hot lists," and a great deal of expediting, had managed to get the parts needed to keep the shipments up to budget. When the manufacturing vice president insisted that they work to the new system and work to the priorities it gave them, inventories increased, shipments fell off, and customer service deteriorated badly. Installing the "execution" phase of a system before correcting the planning phase only results in a more effective means of executing a bad plan.

Company G is another company that did a great many things right. Their application was sound, their users were involved, they weren't oversophisticated and their plans called for cautious step-by-step implementation. Nevertheless, they never got their system working; in fact, they never really got it implemented. This company is simply incapable of operating as a team. Results are elusive and excuses abundant; data processing blames manufacturing, manufacturing blames data processing, marketing blames engineering, engineering blames finance, and the general order of the day is one continual round of "Who Shot John?" This is a case of simply being incapable of getting an organization to get anything accomplished. It certainly is pathetic. All the individuals involved are fine, but their collective efforts always seem to come to nothing.

Company H had a branch warehouse inventory control system developed and installed by their systems man. He was entranced by sophistication and developed a system that was completely unintelligible to anyone but himself. (Even he couldn't understand some parts of it a month after it was on the air!) Many complex decisions were programmed into the computer. These were a big mystery to the users, who assumed that the computer would manage the inventory for them. When inventory went completely out of control, there was no one they could really blame — including the systems man who had long since been promoted to corporate headquarters. Nor was there any way to manage the system. It was very automatic, but not automatic enough to run without human intervention.

The objective in these examples is not to ridicule these companies used to illustrate the causes of systems failure. In every case there were good people within the companies trying hard to make the systems succeed for their company. These specific examples were chosen to show how easy it is to fail. They are representative of the large number of actual company experiences that were examined in culling out the six key reasons for systems failure.

These *six key reasons* were not placed in any significant numerical order (except to establish a rational sequence for the subsequent chapters that address each of these problems). It is worth noting how often reason 3 — system designed by systems people — appears. Nevertheless, even this may be misleading. I personally feel that reason 6 — inability to manage with a system — is really the most universal problem. Today, few companies do enough other things right to allow one to judge whether or not they could have managed with their system. In the future, reason 6 is likely to be the most common reason for systems failure.

It may seem a rather negative approach to search for the key reasons for failure rather than the reasons for success, but this is a necessary exercise in order to separate the "vital few" reasons from the many that are possible. If we read books on computer systems they encourage the designer to use a modular approach, start with the "grand design," reduce clerical effort, and keep paper output to a minimum, as well as frequently mentioning points akin to key reason 3.

The challenge was not to come up with more "good advice" but to boil it down to the essentials. And that is the important point. *Each* of these keys *is essential* if systems are going to succeed. Many companies have failed because they ignored even one key, although in their "adolescent" years most companies — like the companies in our examples — made several errors.

Note, by the way, the number of companies in which serious management problems kept systems from being developed and used properly. Where these types of problems do exist, it is easy — and almost always factual — to observe that the system is inadequate. Company D, for example, operates in fire fighting mode. In spite of the obvious fact that they need better systems badly, until there is a change in management attitude no system will produce results. It's like opening the hood of an ailing car and noticing that the battery is missing. The car certainly needs a battery but once it has a good one there is no guarantee that the car will run. Perhaps there is no rotor in the distributor. The battery was *necessary but not sufficient.*

It is worth mentioning also, that most of the systems that are not really contributing to the companies' operations *are still installed!* And there is little or no intention of ever throwing them out. A few of them are even used as demonstration points by computer salesmen because of their impressive use of hardware. Unfortunately, a good many systems fall into the category of:

Not Good Enough To Use And Not Bad Enough To Throw Out.

But the computer rental and systems maintenance cost goes on and on, in spite of the lack of results.

These six key reasons for systems failure can be avoided and, in fact, must be avoided if we are to have successful systems. If we understand these pitfalls thoroughly, we also understand the six keys to systems success. They are not easy to follow; nor are they obvious. But if they are followed religiously systems can be successful.

It's often a little frightening to see the inexperienced systems man and the inexperienced user heading into a new systems effort. It is somewhat like watching a teenage boy and girl walk down the street together, arms around each other on a bright spring day. In spite of the fact that they see more to criticize than praise in most of the marriages they know, they have supreme confidence that the future will be completely different *for them.* There will be a few problems and easy solutions. Unfortunately, it doesn't work out this way. The goal is well worth attaining, but anybody who underestimates the amount of effort that must be exerted to do the job properly is naive and will be doomed to learn the hard way from sad experience.

WHY BOTHER WITH THE DAMN THINGS...

In 1914, the British government rejected plans for the fastest airplane yet designed — too fast to be used for observation! Thirty-one out of the first forty pilots who flew the airmail between New York and Chicago were killed in crashes. The Empire State Building was built with a Zeppelin mooring mast on top (later used as a television tower).

Any new technology is fraught with gross errors, disasters, and misdirections. As knowledge develops, it feeds on itself and builds exponentially. The standard technology curve, shown in Figure 1, can be applied to any field. If we use the vertical scale to represent speeds of aircraft and the horizontal scale to represent time, it fairly depicts progress from 1903 into the age of rocketships. Explosive power followed the same curve from firecrackers to hydrogen bombs. The computer will do the same. Computers were first used to any extent in business in the late 1950's and the early 1960's. Twelve to fifteen years later would be the equivalent of 1915-1918 in aircraft development. The fact that we have made gross mistakes is no surprise — but *we must learn from these mistakes.*

Or should we bother? Why not pursue business as usual and ignore the computer? Unfortunately, only a few companies can actually do this, because, like most new technology, the computer fulfills — and, yes, even creates — a compelling need. It can provide a significant competitive advantage when used well. And for good reasons.

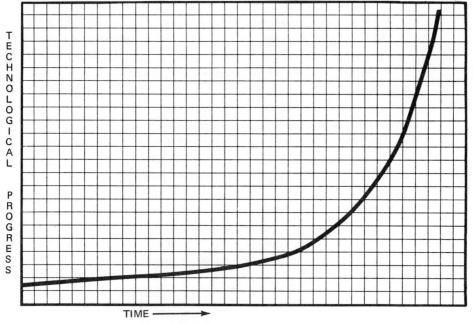

Figure 1. The standard technology curve.

The president of one of this country's most successful companies recalls that they made only one model of their product in 1958, the year he joined the company. Today they make thousands of models. For years they were rich and paid little attention to inventories; today, because of high interest rates, they need better controls. Yet the proliferation and increasing complexity of the product really compounds the control problems.

In the past, most companies used two systems (at least) in most of their operations control areas. Because it was difficult — indeed sometimes virtually impossible — for formal manual systems to provide the right type of information quickly enough to allow people the proper control, they made up for the deficiencies with their own informal systems.

Many companies go through a number of stages with informal systems.

Phase 1 Competent people run the company with informal systems.
        Stanley was in charge of raw material in Company X. He looked into the freight cars and "eye-balled" each department's raw material each morning. When schedules told him about a change in customer requirements, he adjusted his raw material ordering accordingly (he knew which materials were used in every major product and could figure in his head how a schedule change would effect material requirements). But, as more and more materials were added and they were used in more and more products, he had difficulty keeping everything in his head. Fortunately, retirement solved the problem for him — but not for the company — as they entered . . .

Phase 2 More and more people exert more and more effort on the formal system, but the situation drifts out of control.
        The formal system in this company never was very effective. Raw material went into a warehouse and was then distributed to any one of seven different user depart-

ments. Because it was impractical to post inventory activity in and out of the warehouse and in and out of each department manually the formal system only showed one *inventory balance. Material was added to it when received and deducted from it when a department reported consumption. Simple, but really inadequate since frequently one department would run out of material and find that the warehouse had none. Knowing that there was probably some material available in another department, they would call and ask inventory control people where it was. The people who replaced Stan did not do as thorough job of "eye-balling" the shop each day. Foremen were very critical because no one in inventory control "seemed very knowledgeable." Schedules told the expanded force of raw material inventory clerks about impending changes yet they still got caught without material. They simply weren't experienced enough to do the quick mental conversion of schedules to material requirements that Stan did. The "formal" system based all material ordering on past usage only. As costs and inventories went up and material shortages increased people exerted extreme efforts to control, but the "system" could not control anymore. In fact, the "system" had retired! They are soon likely to enter . . .*

Phase 3   The situation is out of control.
Everyone is frustrated at their lack of ability to perform. Morale drops along with performance and everyone blames everyone else in an orgy of fingerpointing. Management fires a few people, hires a few new ones, and seems incapable of finding anyone who can "walk on water!"

The problem described above is not unusual. But transition through these phases seems to happen insidiously. Few of the principals seem to understand what has happened: *it is no longer possible to control the business without a formal system.*

Late in 1969, I chose three companies to watch closely in 1970. Their selection was based on their past successes in the use of computer systems in manufacturing control. Interestingly enough, each of them made record profits in 1970. A year when their competitors suffered serious, and in some cases disasterous, effects from the business recession. The point is very simple: *companies that use computer systems to manage, tend to manage better.*

Is this cause, or is it effect? Probably both. Because they manage well, they see the potential for better management through better systems. Because they are good managers, they are more successful in developing and installing successful computer systems. These better systems then help them to manage better. The rich get richer . . . .

If the Watsons of IBM had been marketing airplanes, they probably would have had one in everyone's garage in 1927. Certainly their enthusiastic marketing approaches have filled their salesmen and customers with a conviction that the computer *can* help them!

And that guy with an airplane in his garage may have a monkey on his back, or he may have an opportunity to get a real jump on competition. IBM's aggressive, imaginative — and usually sincere — marketing approaches have certainly sold computers to many companies not yet ready to use them. But this may not be altogether a bad thing. Most businesses have got the computer, but they have also got the problems. The challenge is to learn how to use computer systems to help *people* control businesses more effectively.

2

The Conspiracy
for Sophistication

"They believed in short that they held in their steady hands the candle that would light the world. We have inherited this belief, and it has helped and hurt us."

Arthur Miller, *THE CRUCIBLE*

WHO SAID SOPHISTICATION WAS GOOD?

Oversophistication has been the downfall of many a system. The most successful systems tend to be essentially quite simple. When systems are too sophisticated, the user does not understand them and tends either to follow them blindly or ignore them completely and develop his own informal subsystems. Why, then, are so many people convinced that it is desirable to be sophisticated?

Let's start by looking at the meaning of the word *sophisticated*. There has been an insidious change in connotation creeping into the word. Back in 1958, about the time the computer era

19

really began for manufacturing companies, the American College Dictionary gave the following definition:

Sophisticate: 1) to make less natural, simple or ingenuous; to make worldly-wise; 2) to mislead or pervert; 3) to use sophistry, quibble.

By 1963, the Merriam Webster Dictionary defines *Sophisticate:*

1) to alter deceptively; especially adulterate; 2) to deprive of genuineness, naturalness or simplicity, especially to deprive of naivety and make worldly-wise, disillusion; 3) to make complicated or complex, refine.

They then go on to define the adjective *Sophisticated:*

1) not in a natural pure original state, adulterated; 2) deprived of native or original simplicity as: (a) highly complicated, (b) worldly-wise, knowing; 3) devoid of grossness, subtle as: (a) finely experienced and aware, (b) intellectually appealing.

Isn't it interesting to watch the progress of that word in the computer age. Just as the word progressed in history: the word *sophia* originally meant intelligence, wisdom; *sophistry* generally carries the connotation of misused intelligence. Sophisticate at the beginning of the computer age meant to adulterate, but today when we speak of a *sophisticated computer system* most people mean *advanced* or *refined* — although, perhaps, perverted and adulterated would be an appropriate description for many. "Intellectually appealing" is a particularly applicable description of many of today's least successful systems.[1]

A good word for the businessman to exercise more frequently is the word *effective.* Try substituting it for *sophisticated* as you

---

[1] When I use the word "sophisticated" in this book, I will always mean *intellectually appealing.* To me the word is *bad!*

hear people describe "sophisticated systems." Are they effective systems — or just intellectually appealing?

There is a fine line between *sophisticated* and *effective*. A material requirements planning system, for example, is not in itself sophisticated. The computer is given an assembly schedule. It checks the bill of material (parts list) file to determine what parts are needed to make the assemblies scheduled. It then checks the inventory file to see if these parts are on order with the right priority. If not, it indicates to a planner which parts must be ordered or rescheduled.

This is simply a formal system to do what the foremen and expeditors were always trying to do with an informal system. It *can* be made sophisticated, however. The designer could add some complex lot-sizing calculations like "Part Period Balancing with Look-Ahead/Look-Back" or the "Wagner/Whitin Algorithm."[2]

These are attempts to mathematically optimize the lot-size by various calculations involving the following basic data:

1. The forecast of future demand.
2. Unit cost of the item.
3. Machine set-up cost.
4. Inventory carrying cost.

Forecasts are usually wrong, by definition. Unit costs and machine set-up costs (if available!) are approximations at best. Almost no one claims to know what it really costs in total to carry inventory; we can only estimate a reasonable figure. But isn't it fun to develop a formula that can massage an error and an approximation and an estimate to get precise results!

But then the systems designer — not quite sure that he has covered all the bases — will tell the inventory planner to check and approve the orders the computer system generates! The poor planner is unlikely to understand the computations and logic involved.

---

[2] These are both real techniques, believe it or not!

More important, he is closer to the real world and probably suspects that a simpler approach for arriving at what is essentially an approximation would work every bit as well. He recognizes the sophisticated approach for what it is: intellectually appealing. But only to the designer — not to the user.

A book could be written citing case after case where systems designers have chosen sophisticated techniques when simpler ones would have sufficed. Why? *Because its more glamorous to be sophisticated!* The boys at the technical society will be more impressed. Might even get a paper published in *Management Science.*

This type of immature thinking is not uncommon but it certainly does not represent a sound business attitude. Fortunately, not all systems designers and data processing people have been seduced by the romance of the hardware and the siren call of sophistication. But it is hard to resist the temptation to razzle-dazzle the less gifted mortals with sophisticated achievements.

When business historians look back at the twenty-year period following World War II they are likely to label it "The Age of Naive Sophistication." During this period everything sophisticated was "good"; everything unsophisticated was bad. Anyone who was against the more sophisticated approach was "impossibly dull." Why have we then been bombarded with propaganda on sophistication? Why has a cult of sophistication tended to grow up in the United States? For two reasons:

1. It *is* intellectually appealing; and
2. While it may not be in the best interests of the businessman, it does serve the interests of many groups that influence him.

WHATEVER BECAME OF OPERATIONS RESEARCH?

The application of more scientific, analytical, mathematical techniques to problems where probability and optimum use of limited resources is involved got a good deal of attention during World War II when the English application of "Operational Research" received widespread publicity. The idea was to have some scientists sitting in the group of military personnel to lend their expertise in solving difficult problems such as the optimum size for convoys, the allocation of limited numbers of aircraft to defense versus offense, etc.

After the War, Operations Research came into its own in the United States. A great deal of attention was put to applying Operations Research techniques to business problems such as production and inventory control, problems where probability is the order of the day in making forecasts and where the use of limited resources like inventory is a constant concern. Some of the influence of Operations Research has been quite positive. Many of the areas of business had been neglected and operated by seat-of-the-pants methods for too many years.

As with many good ideas, however, perversion set in rather quickly and Operations Research seems to be no longer in vogue. Very few companies have Operations Research departments anymore and, in fact, most of the Operations Research people now seem to prefer to call it "Management Science." Probably to get away from the bad connotations of the old name. To many businessmen, Operations Research is the sophistry of the business age.

What is wrong with Operations Research and why has it failed to accomplish all the great feats forecast for it? A number of things have happened. For one thing, the old concept of the "team" seems to have gotten lost. Too many Operations Researchers have found it much more entertaining to communicate with each other rather than to communicate with managers who have forgotten most of the calculus they ever knew. They have also often found developing elegant solutions to trivial problems more challenging than working on the real business problems. They start out with the assumption that the solution is going to be a complex mathematical one and often develop elaborate inventory models that are difficult to apply in a company where the managers have not yet figured out how to keep the inventory-on-hand, balance record correct. Nevertheless, the lack of practical application of these techniques is not a deterrent to widespread discussion about them and, in fact, their incorporation into a great deal of the business college curricula.

For comments on the current condition of Operations Research, let's turn to one of the most eminent Operations Researchers of today, J. W. Forester. (Mr. Forester developed the concept of Industrial Dynamics and is Professor of Management at the Massachusetts Institute of Technology.) In an article in *The New York Times* (January 11, 1970) discussing the reasons why Operations Researchers have not been successful, he says:

> "Their focus is more mathematical than operational. Most of the research on rules for decision making originates from men with little background in management practice or political leadership. Management science and mathematical economics have become closed academic societies where teachers teach students to become teachers with little intrusion by outside reality. . . . Professional papers are written for a 'public' that will read for the display of mathematical skill rather than for practical utility."

Forester goes on to say:

> "Mathematics is so weak when faced with the complexity and nonlinearity of real situations that the simplifying assumptions have forced the work outside the realm of major problems. The search for professional security has held the field to trivial objectives."

Books and books and books have been written on the kinds of subjects that Mr. Forester describes. Most of them were written by men not honest or realistic enough to make the kind of comments that Hadley and Whitin make in the preface to their book, *Analysis of Inventory Systems:*[3]

---

[3] Englewood Cliffs, New Jersey: Prentice-Hall, Inc., 1963.

"An increasing number of individuals are working with inventory models because they present interesting theoretical problems in mathematics. For such individuals, practical application is not a major objective although there is the possibility that their theoretical work may be helpful in practice at some future time."

Messrs. Hadley and Whitin go on to say:

"The material treated in this book is concerned almost exclusively with the determination of optimal operating doctrines, for systems consisting of a single stocking point and a single source of supply. The reasons for doing this are (1) many practical problems fall into this category, (2) many interesting mathematical problems arise when attention is restricted to these relatively simple systems, and (3) it is extremely difficult to determine optimal operating doctrines for more complex systems."

Cheers for Hadley and Whitin. While the attention currently being given theoretical problems is out of all proportion to their educational and business value, honesty is always impressive. It's a pity that some of the other authors of articles and books have not seen fit to call people's attention to their real objectives as clearly as Messrs. Hadley and Whitin have. It is hard to talk about Operations Research without talking about our educational system. While these activities are perpetuated by professional societies they were — and still *are* — being spawned in many of our colleges.

John Kenneth Galbraith, in his book *The New Industrial State*,[4] had an interesting comment about education when he said:

"Much economic instruction and notably so in such fields as advanced theory, foreign trade and monetary policy, depends not on the relevance of the subject matter but on the existence of an intellectually preoccupying theory."

This is true of many courses in production management at the college level, although certainly not of all; it is a credit to a

---

[4] New York, N.Y.: New American Library, 1968.

number of colleges that they are trying to take a more practical approach. Nevertheless, while many of the colleges are truly concerned about the relevancy of the material they teach, they are bucking the academic heirarchy. Practical programs of education are often considered "vocational" in Academia and rate low on the prestige totem pole. Thus, some academic people refer to the schools that teach highly irrelevant mathematical techniques as the "strong (good word!) schools." As if the value of the course content were to be judged on the level of mathematics demonstrated!

Since it's easier to learn and teach mathematics — a field in which principles and techniques have been identified — the worship of those courses most mathematical (referred to in Academia as "rigorous courses") is convenient. It also avoids the necessity for having to try to learn and teach the subject of business, which is far less structured and often beyond the experience of the teachers.

Linear programming — a mathematical optimizing technique — is a good case in point. There are several books on the subject and numerous articles. A book on Production Control which did not discuss it as a technique for optimizing the assignment of jobs to machines when alternatives are available would not be acceptable to many college professors. Yet the technique has had few known successful applications to this problem in the real world! One plant that tried it rapidly switched to a simpler approach; others have not bothered with it because it just is not a very useful technique in this application (it has had *limited* use in other applications). Nevertheless, it is taught by most colleges; primarily because it is a rigorous, intellectually challenging, and eminently teachable subject. When reminded of the very, very few places where this technique really applies, the college professor's normal reaction is to blame the general ignorance of the businessman who is "just too dull-witted" and doesn't understand all this good stuff!

We've been graduating students chock full of Operations Research techniques for over twenty years now. Since there are very, very few successful (profitable) Operations Research applications in business, something must be wrong. It can't *just* be the dull-witted businessman — surely all of these graduates couldn't have gone back to teaching!

The fact that very little serious non-mathematical literature has been available on business has also encouraged the teaching of "sophisticated" material at the college level. Much of what has been written on production management, for example, of a non-mathematical type is pure drivel. At least the instructor does see some "meat" in the mathematics. One cannot help but sympathize a little bit with these "strong" schools and their supporters. But what of the graduates of these courses? What do they do with the almost totally irrelevant knowledge that they now have?

Some of them will look for jobs in Operations Research — a dwindling field. Others will get more mundane jobs and rapidly learn to disdain the people who really run business because they sure don't run it the way it was taught in school. They will search, usually in vain, for problems to fit the solutions they have learned. By belonging to a scientific, technical society, they can escape from reality by getting out to dinner once a month and discussing their hobby. (Usually the business will pay for this too!) Eventually, many of these students will get frustrated with business and go back to teaching to perpetuate the intellectual incest. Some, hopefully, may adjust to the real world in spite of their education.

Unfortunately, this is too often the exception. As Professor J. Sterling Livingston pointed out, "if academic achievement is equated with success in business, the well-educated manager is a myth." And also, ". . . much management education is, in fact, miseducation. . . ."[5]

Peter Drucker in *The Age of Discontinuity*[6] makes a number of interesting comments on this subject. Here are a few:

"Education has become too important to be left to the educators." (Page 313.)

---

[5] "The Myth Of the Well-Educated Manager," *Harvard Business Review*, January-February, 1971.

[6] New York, N.Y.: Harper & Row, Publishers, 1968.

"Yesterday's educators had no choice but to extend the only school they had, the only school they knew... the result is a school that deforms rather than forms." (Page 317.)

"We need only a small number of people who are purely theoretical, but we need an infinite number of people capable of using theory as the basis of skill for practical application of work." (Page 318.)

"We need to punch big holes in the diploma curtain through which the able and ambitious can move, even though they have not sat long enough on school benches to satisfy the schoolmaster's requirements." (Page 332.)

Drucker goes on to point out that education is our least productive enterprise and that, if the current trend continues, within a small number of years everybody will be in education and nobody will be working for a living!

We get some really foolish spinoffs from this pretense that irrelevant mathematical elegance is a worthy pursuit for a large number of people. Job shop simulators, for example, have been programmed on computers, and while there are some practical problems they can be used to address, this is seldom what happens. Most of them are used in pursuit of absolutely irrelevant questions such as "which static dispatching rule is the best one to use." Most companies today wouldn't think of using a static dispatching rule like "do the oldest job first" or "do the job with the least processing time on it first," yet literally millions of dollars have been spent on this type of simulation and there are men whose life's work revolves around these mock-heroic studies which are primarily just mental diddling by computer.

Why haven't we recognized how irrelevant, useless, and even harmful this educational path is? Probably for a number of reasons. Rudolf Flesch said it well:[7]

"The ordinary citizen with his customary reverence for everything that is printed and his awe of everything that is unintelligible has no way of knowing when to bow his head and when to say 'nuts!' "[8]

---

[7] *The Art of Readable Writing*, New York, N.Y.: Collier Books, 1962.

[8] I prefer *fantastic*.

That's part of the problem. Most businessmen have left the problem of education to educators — those least qualified to really understand business education. They go off to business school sponsored education programs that are almost totally irrelevant and return with a warm feeling that they've done something that should somehow vaguely result in "improvement of the mind." Then they encourage others to go and sit through the same rigorous hardships and join their little club of "intellectuals"!

The tragedy of this worship of sophistication was brought home to me recently when a young man of great talent and potential told me that he was going into accounting in a public utility after he graduated from his state university. I asked him why he didn't get into manufacturing (betraying my own prejudices). His answer was straight and to the point: "I wanted to, but I was weak in third-order differential equations and, therefore, couldn't get into the production management courses in my university." Fantastic!

LET'S ALL BLAME THE COMPUTER SALESMAN

There has been a tendency on the part of the computer salesman to favor the complex. This is a throwback to the early days of computers, when one of the standard sales techniques was to demonstrate a complex mathematical technique and then say "Aha! Let's see you do *that* without a computer!"

Very few people in a computer company have ever worked in the type of company they are supposed to be teaching and designing applications for. Most of the high-level executives in computer companies have very little knowledge of the practical applications of their hardware and generally favor anything sophisticated because it looks "computerish." "Good" from a computer marketing point of view!

The computer companies have certainly helped perpetuate the cult of sophistication for a number of reasons. For one thing, they have not been, in many cases, discriminating enough to recognize what nonsense most sophistication truly is. For another, they tend to equate sophistication with progress because they are exposed to a great deal of Operations Research literature and indeed seem to be one of the few industries left that still hires any real number of Operations Research trained people.

Fortunately, there has been a trend toward more useful applications lately. A number of recent computer application programs, such as bill-of-material processors and requirements planning programs, *are* practical and oriented toward real business problems. While credit is due for these efforts, these companies have to be extremely careful that they are not mislead by the sophisticates. They often seem to outnumber the practical people and many of them are quite glib and make their theories sound quite plausible. They can show you cases where elegant systems are "installed," and if you go no farther than the data processing room you would have every reason to believe them. If you talk to responsible line operating people and check for real results, the nonsense of the sophisticates becomes transparent.

The computer salesman was part of the conspiracy for sophistication in the past, but he certainly was not the cause. He was surrounded by people, including many of his customers, who believed that *sophisticated* meant "good" and tended to believe it himself after awhile. Many experienced computer salesmen today have also matured and abandoned the worship of sophistication because they recognize it as self-defeating.

OTHER MEMBERS OF THE CONSPIRACY

The first requirement most management people check when looking for a Data Processing or Systems Manager is his technical knowledge. This is primarily because they are in awe of the computer area and overestimate the importance of technical expertise in managing it. The fact is that the most important qualifications a good Data Processing/Systems Manager can have are management skills.

By putting people who are mainly technically oriented in charge of data processing and systems, management has made two mistakes:

1. They have helped to perpetuate the problem of having the identification and selection of new computer applications in the hands of *computer specialists.*
2. They have made the data processing and systems managers virtually umpromotable because they are specialists.

As a result, these people often get little enjoyment out of business and identify better with the people in their technical societies. Frequently these groups serve as a vehicle to glorify the man with the latest in sophisticated applications and hardware. "Profits" and things like that are not a major topic of discussion at these meetings.

The influences on data processing and systems people are insidious. Pick up a data processing magazine. Read the articles. Most of them are "application independent." They are not at all concerned with *what* is being done, but only with *how* it is being done. Is it any wonder that the data processing and systems people too often become fascinated with the hardware and equate progress with having more sophisticated systems and hardware in the company?

The data processing manager's role is often exactly the same as the computer salesman's role. In many cases he is a stronger and more persistent salesman than the man employed by the computer manufacturer. More and more hardware and more and more systems people, with more and more programmers every year. And management is at fault. Management has failed to make these people part of the company team. They have not been convinced of the value and satisfaction a man can get from participating in running a business.

They sense, often unconsciously, that by enhancing their technical skills they are giving themselves a means to advancement.

As a consequence, they easily become entranced with the glamour of systems and hardware as *ends* rather than *means*. This is easy to do, since data processing salaries are largely related to the complexity of the hardware and software that a man has used, as well as the number of people he has managed. It is difficult for a man who has been put in an unpromotable position by management not to have thoughts of his resumé cross his mind occasionally.

These people can easily become part of the conspiracy for sophistication because all around them people are applauding it and equating it with progress and advancement. They often see it as a way to develop more complex computer applications to help justify bigger computer systems. The solution to this problem is apparent but ignored in most companies: *Get the data processing and systems people into the mainstream of management.* Move users into systems jobs and systems people into user's jobs. Take the man you would like to see running the data processing department someday and let him work for a year as a foreman. You'll soon learn whether he is able to manage or not. If he cannot, *don't* put him in charge of data processing, because the most important aspects of that job are not technical. Later, if he succeeds as manager of data processing he will be promotable — in the meantime, he can lead his people as a manager oriented toward *your business.*

Too often management has kept data processing and systems people out of the mainstream and thereby failed to utilize one of the greatest resources the company has. Because these have been the glamour occupations some extremely capable people are in systems and data processing. They are anxious to see the company improve. They are used to real hard work — take a look at them when they are getting a new system on the air; time and effort mean nothing. But management needs to get a message to some of them by word and deed:

Sophistication is not a legitimate business objective.

In the future we need systems people who are more management oriented. We need management people who are more systems oriented, and, above all, we need to recognize that computer systems are not toys for the technician, but are tools for the managers.

AND *THEN* WE HAVE THE CONSULTANTS

And what about the consultants? There are hundreds of them, and they have been around for many years. Yet you must look far and wide to find successful systems that *they* have installed.

The computer manufacturer calls his representative a "salesman," and he tells people that this man is paid on commission when he can convince the customer to buy or rent a machine. The consulting firm has a number of people whom they call "principals," "vice presidents," etc., and who are primarily in the business of selling the services of "resident" consultants. These principals and vice presidents usually get paid a "bonus" for the number of days they can rent their "resident consultants" out. Let's face one fact: Consulting is a very commercial enterprise as it is practiced by most institutional consulting firms; the business consists of renting bodies.

This is not to say that there are not some very professional consultants. There are also a few thieves and a few incompetents. The vast majority of them are more successful at making profits for themselves than for their clients and most of their "residents" are average people with no more talent than some of the client's people.

How can these people's services be sold then? Easy. Hire graduates of the sophisticated schools[9] and peddle sophistication as hard as you can!

---

[9] In his article, "The Myth of the Well-Educated Manager," (see reference, page 27), Professor Livingstone points out that Harvard Business School M.B.A.'s, who have a generally disappointing record in business, tend more and more to join consulting firms. He goes on to point out: "As Charlie Brown prophetically observed in a Peanuts cartoon strip in which he is standing on the pitcher's mound surrounded by his players, all of whom are telling him what to do at a critical point in a baseball game: The world is filled with people who are anxious to act in an advisory capacity."

One prominent company called a well-known consultant in to do a "job" for them. The "residents" were practically all M.B.A.'s from a prominent and very sophisticated business school. Result: Plenty of "billing days" for the consultant and three books of unintelligible elegant trash for the client.

Sophistication is good business for the consultant — the vice president of a large, nationally known consulting firm proudly proclaims his company's expertise in "complex" business systems. His general approach conveys the idea that ordinary mortals probably could not learn enough about the really sophisticated techniques to install them without a large dose of his company's resident consulting. Sophistication is good for *his* business. Call him whenever you would like to "rent-a-wizard!"

THE CASE AGAINST SOPHISTICATION

Until such time as completely reliable automatic systems can be developed, it is important to avoid automating just enough to force the user to learn a great deal more about the sophisticated system in order to control. Consider the automatic choke that was introduced in the mid-1930's. When automobiles had hand chokes it was a pretty simple matter to pull out the choke and turn on the starter to start the car, then push the choke in after the car started running. With the advent of the early, unreliable automatic chokes, anyone who wanted to operate his car consistently had to learn how to open the hood, take the air cleaner off, reach in and if the choke valve was closed, open it; if it was open, close it, put the air cleaner back on, close the hood, get back in and start the car. Any junior mechanic could master the technique quite simply! Obviously, when automatic chokes became almost 100 percent reliable, they were a valuable addition to the automobile.

We really need to develop a type of value analysis for systems design. First the systems designers should ask:

Is the system going to require human intervention and judgment?

Any system that cannot reliably follow rigid sets of rules under all conditions is going to require human intervention. For example, there are almost no inventory systems where computers really do the ordering. Strikes, one-time-only price breaks, short-term quality problems, price increases, and many other conditions could affect the decision. The systems designer should remember that when the human must be responsible, the level of sophistication can easily baffle the user. As one company recently pointed out: "No single element in our system is complex, but in total it is difficult for the users to understand and use the system well."

The technically oriented systems designer is often ready to add one more bell or whistle to the system because "it's no problem to do that." In fact, his technician's knowledge tells him that this will even help exercise the computer's circuitry a little more, since computers can always do more calculations while the printer speed or some other input or output function is the bottleneck.

But this is a serious mistake. The real test of value is not the computer's ability to handle the added sophistication, but the user's. Whenever any more sophistication is being considered, make these tests of systems value analysis:

1. Will it really be more *effective* or is it primarily intellectually appealing?

2. When considering the function and significance of this element in the real world, is this an area that is truly worth fine tuning?

3. Identify the last 20 percent of sophistication that will generate 80 percent of the system cost and confusion.

4. What will the extra sophistication cost in user understanding of this part of the system? Of the overall system?

5. Is there a simpler way to do it?

Let's consider an example. One of the recent and valid ideas in production and inventory management is the concept of "dynamic priorities." The idea behind it is simple and valid: In any factory the real priorities change after a job has been released to the factory. It is not valid to put a required date on a shop order that will be in the factory for six weeks, for example, and assume that priorities will not change.

As a consequence, with the advent of the computer, the general practice is to recalculate required dates for items periodically, and to use some sort of dispatch list that goes out to the factory, usually on a daily basis, to communicate these priorities to production control and factory supervision personnel. With an order point system, this can be done by recalculating the average rate of use and, perhaps once a week, dividing this into the inventory on hand in order to predict when stock will run out. Requirements planning systems also recalculate priorities, usually on a weekly basis or more frequently.

This is excellent. Here is a great step forward in being able to make the formal system do what the informal system struggled inefficiently and ineffectively to do in the past: Keep realistic requirement dates on shop orders. But the idea was no sooner suggested than someone had figured out how to add a little bit of sophistication to it. Instead of just recalculating the due date for the item and moving the schedule in each work center forward or back accordingly, why not put this all into one simple ratio — often called Critical Ratio. In one version of this technique, a simple priority number is calculated based on the amount of time left between today and the required date for the job, and the amount of time originally scheduled for remaining operations.

Consider a job that is due to be completed in eight working days and the job is sitting at operation number 3. There are a number of remaining operations. When the job was originally scheduled it was planned to allow twelve working days to perform these opera-tions. Thus, the Critical Ratio becomes:

Time remaining to due date = 8 days

"Work" remaining $\quad = 12$ days = Critical Ratio $\frac{8}{12} = 0.67$

This is a little bit more complicated than just changing re-quirement dates, but it can be argued that there is some superior-ity in calculating a simple priority number rather than just chang-ing the schedule dates as requirement dates change and printing these out on the computer. Nevertheless, some sophistication has been added.

But wait until some of the systems "sophisticates" get their hands on even this technique! In one company, a dispatching system was designed using the Critical Ratio approach. A great many "bells and whistles" were added, however. One of these calculations is called the "tie breaker." (Ties exist when two prior-ities are equal. It never occurred to them that they might let the foreman or dispatcher choose either job!) There are many other calculations. The resulting algorithm is so complex that it has been named after its developer, since only he understands it! Of course the priority rules can't recognize *all* contingencies in a real-world factory so the foremen are also told to be sure to use "good judgment." Can you imagine how much judgment they will use in interpreting a seven-digit priority number based on an algorithm only a mathematician could understand!

And how much significance does it have in the system? It's more important to put the emphasis on revising priorities to keep them realistic! If these requirement dates are kept correct, 99 percent of the real value in the factory will probably result. The example above is an excellent case of a technique that has been "deprived of its native simplicity." The systems men who spent many long hours on this intellectually challenging assignment would have been far better off to have gone into the factory and found out what the real world is like![10]

In the real factory, there are things changing day-to-day that represent even more compelling reasons for changing priority than any computer can respond to. Machines break down, tools don't work properly, a trained operator isn't available, one of the most important customers is going to shut down if he doesn't get an emergency shipment that he just called in about this morning, etc. The foreman knows that these things are going to happen and when the systems man comes down with his latest exercise in pseudo-sophistication, it's very difficult for shop people to take him seriously.

Consider another company in contrast. They designed a system that was similar in concept but considerably different in design. They, too, used Critical Ratio but they showed the actual time remaining and work remaining on the dispatch list in addition to the Critical Ratio. They did this so that the foreman could see where the number came from. A good example of "system transparency" (more about this in Chapter 5). Their dispatch list goes to people who note in pencil on the computer printout whether jobs are running, waiting for tools, etc. When they have priority "ties," they tell the foreman and dispatchers to "pick either job." This second company, incidentally, designed and installed their system in about nine months with a minimum of systems and programming time. The foremen like it and it works. The first system with all the sophistication in it has taken four times as long

---

[10] There have been some interesting theoretical treatises written on the subject of priority rules. They usually cite some simulations where rules such as "minimum slack time," Critical Ratio, "slack time per operation," and other rules are compared. It never seems to occur to these sophisticates to run a real-world test to determine whether or not these priority rules really have any value! I know of two companies, for example, with quite comparable production and inventory control systems. Both do an excellent job of re-planning priorities to keep them up to date. One just changes scheduled dates while the other changes scheduled dates and calculates a Critical Ratio. I cannot discern any performance superiority at the second company!

to get on the air. It hasn't worked yet and there is some serious doubt that it ever will without some dramatic revisions.

These examples are cited, not to be critical of the people involved so much as to show how difficult it is to keep people on the track and away from useless and harmful sophistication. It *is* glamorous and intellectually appealing!

A good system is designed to best use the abilities of the computer and the human being. The second system mentioned above, for example, lets the computer recalculate priorities — something a human being could not do. It then gives this information to the human being, recognizing that humans are extremely flexible and can cope with unstructured, constantly changing situations far better than a computer can. Some systems designers, particularly the inexperienced and naive, will try — even though they know they can't build 100 percent logic into the computer — to build in as much logic as possible, in the hopes that this will help the user. The fact is that it does just the opposite. If 90 percent of the logic is built into the computer and 10 percent is left out, the user must know *which* 10 percent was left out. If 95 percent was built in and 5 percent left out, a higher level of knowledge will be required in order to use the system intelligently. If 98 percent of the decisions are built in and 2 percent are left out, probably only the systems man himself would be capable of running the system — and this would be a just punishment for him.

The importance of developing unsophisticated systems cannot be overemphasized. It isn't just the cost, it isn't just the unbusinesslike mental diddling involved. The most important contributions of simplicity to a system are in installation, in maintaining the integrity of the system, in giving the users control, and probably, most important, in system continuity. The simpler the system is, the easier it can be installed, maintained, and continued because the users understand it and see it as a tool to help them, rather than as a monster that they constantly have to outwit. Sophistication, even if it appears to be free, is a very expensive perversion that has been the downfall of many a system. Very few systems have failed because they weren't sophisticated enough.

Back in 1958, IBM introduced a concept called MOS. This was to be a total management operating system all built around a single data base. Of course, nobody ever managed to install anything like this concept! In 1964, IBM introduced the Bill of Material Processor, a way to get bills of material and inventory files, for example, on a computer so that they could be maintained and cross-referenced properly. This was a considerably less ambitious approach than trying to install a total MOS! In 1971, there is a tremendous amount of interest in the United States in developing better stockroom integrity so that inventory records can be maintained more accurately. Isn't it interesting to see how the focus has gone from the esoteric to the fundamental and significant parts of the problem.

Why isn't sophistication completely out of vogue? Well, it is appealing and often profitable for the "Operations Research-Systems/Data Processing-Consulting-Academia" people. They have an immensely powerful propaganda machine, since each supports the others' exaggerations of the truth. Magazines, technical societies, and technical journals, in addition to their positive contributions, all must bear the responsibility for perpetuating this naive approach. The participants in the conspiracy for sophistication have a set of pre-established beliefs (computers, Operations Research, Management Information Systems, rigorous college courses, etc., are all *good* per se), and selective interpretation of the facts continues to bolster their convictions.

Fortunately, there are signs that the naive and immature preoccupation with sophistication as an end in itself is on the wane. Perhaps now more companies will be able to put these childish pursuits behind them and get serious about developing practical systems to solve real business problems.

3

Potential
Profitable Applications

"The lead companies have also put the computer to work on the crucial decisions of the business: in sales forecasting, in manpower and production scheduling, in inventory management."[1]

WHAT CAN MY COMPUTER DO?

What a great job the technicians have done in creating a computer "mystique." The executive was never too concerned about the details of the chemical reactions that took place to make certain compounds the company sold, nor was he terribly concerned over the mechanical and hydraulic, as well as electronic, principles involved in the operations of machine tools that cost thousands of dollars. But suddenly, the computer technicians have sold him a

---

[1] *Getting the Most Out of Your Computer*, McKinsey & Company, Inc., 1963.

bill of goods that he must understand how the computer works "because its influence is all pervasive."[2] So we send him off to a computer school. Obviously, computer schools are developed by computer technicians. After many hours of hard work the executive understands that a computer works in binary arithmetic rather than decimal arithmetic, because it's easier to detect on and off conditions than to detect ten variations of on and off in an electronic device. He even plays the role of programmer and learns what the programmer's job is like in his company. Supposedly, this should give him great insight into using the computer intelligently!

Ask the typical technician what you need to know about the job and he will usually tell you everything he knows. Technical people are not particularly well suited to separating the vital from the trivial and practically all of their body of knowledge seems to them to be vital for the manager to understand, in addition to the knowledge that he has about his particular function. They also enjoy communicating back and forth in a special shorthand. This is extremely practical for them. One man might say to another, "Are you using PICS?" The reply might be, "Only the RPS module and BOMP." The next question might be "Under DOS?" The answer, "Well, really we're using CFMS under OS." A great deal of information has been conveyed between two technicians. When

---

[2] An article that appeared in one of the computer magazines (*Business Automation*, November 15, 1970) is a great example of this condescending attitude. It is titled "Has Top Management Failed the Computer?" The article states:

"Thus, senior management's greatest challenge obviously will be in his own self-education in the sophistication [sic] area of the computer."

"Management certainly must find better justification for its own communications problem."

The lead article in this same issue is the typical propaganda article aggrandizing the role of the technician: "Information Science Needs an Identity." The sincere myopia of the technical types who really believe this type of nonsense is pathetic. Their lack of a real business perspective is deplorably naive.

they start using this same shorthand in front of the non-technically oriented, they are just plain showing off and contributing once more to the great "mystique" of the computer.

This isn't to say that the manager doesn't need to understand *what* the computer can do. It *is* an all-pervasive tool. Most managers work primarily with information, and the computer manipulates information. But what he really needs to know about *how* the computer works is very limited indeed, and when technicians create a "mystique" around the machine — a barrier for the manager — they not only make him dependent upon them, but they also seriously impair his ability to make intelligent decisions about the use of the computer. When they send him off to a school where he learns little of value and has trouble separating it from a mass of technical trivia, they have done little for him. He has been taught a great deal about *how* a computer does things in the hope that he will — perhaps by osmosis — gain a little insight into *what* it can do.

Too often his knowledge just generates awe. Imagine an executive spending three days studying the theory of rotary metal cutting and how a screw machine works. Then give him two evenings to try setting up an eight-spindle automatic. He'd come back damned impressed with his screw machine set-up men, but not really much smarter from a business point of view.

What does the executive really need to know? Very little about *how* the computer does things. He needs to understand *what* it can do and, most important, what are the payoff *applications* in his business.

Basically a computer is a machine that is capable of manipulating vast amounts of data at extremely high speeds. Can it forecast an election? Well, after a fashion. All it really does is process data following some rules like: "If 10 percent of the returns are in from district 7 and the incumbent has a 2 to 1 lead, he has a 9 to 1 chance of being elected." These rules were established by analyzing past election trends (probably with the aid of a computer) and programming them into the machine.

Can it help to control inventory? Yes. It can maintain inventory balances and follow ordering rules much as a human would. Inventory records are kept in files (usually *disc* or *tape)* rather than on paper. They are updated typically by punching data into a card and putting it into the machine. Following a set of procedures (the *program),* the computer will process this data against the data already in its files (add a *receipt* to the inventory *file)* and generate prescribed output such as a stock status report.

Setting up a computer system is very much like setting up a manual system. If there had been no inventory records or system for raw material inventory control, it would be necessary to set one up. Assume that a company had raw material but that there were no inventory records and no formal way of replenishing inventory. Let's say that the warehouse foreman tried to reorder inventory based on his best guesses and looking at the physical inventory in the warehouse occasionally. Then it was decided to set up a manual inventory control system, establish stock record cards, and teach an inventory clerk how to order this material. The following steps would have to be taken:

1. Set up an inventory record file.
2. Define what the input to that file — such as receipts and withdrawals — would look like and where the significant information would appear on the input documents.
3. Define the output that would be required, such as purchase requisitions, manufacturing orders, stock status reports, transaction histories, etc.
4. Give a clerk the instructions — the equivalent of a program — to run the system.

In general, the same type of thing has to be done in setting up a computer system. The output from the program must be defined, the basic files and input documents defined, and after the general logic of the system has been developed, a program must be written. The program provides the instructions to activate the circuits in the computer to perform certain functions.

Combinations of letters and numbers activate particular circuits within the computer to perform these functions. These letters and numbers are the actual "code" of the program. Each computer has its own "machine code" that is required to activate its internal circuitry. This code is very difficult for the user to work with since it makes no sense at all to the human being. Because machine code is so difficult to work with, practically no one uses it today. Almost all programs are written in programming "languages" such as COBOL (*CO*mmon *B*usiness *O*riented *Lan*guage) or FORTRAN (*FOR*mula *TRAN*slation) which must then be translated into machine code. The COBOL program, for example, must be run against a COBOL "compiler" (or translater program) which then creates the actual program in machine code that the computer will use. Figure 2 shows a COBOL program sheet for part of a simple inventory transaction system. The instructions are almost self-explanatory. After opening the inventory files and the input file, the computer reads a card and, if this is the last card, it will go to a set of instructions entitled "Job Finished" (not shown on this program sheet). The first step is, obviously, to determine whether or not the transaction is a withdrawal or a receipt. The withdrawal and receipt routines are also shown. The expression "display master card" means that the information on the master record should be printed out with the label *before change*. The quotation marks in the program tell the computer that these particular words are to be printed on the output report.

The balance of the instructions are pretty much self-explanatory. Obviously, this is not the entire program but it shows the procedure division of a very simple inventory transaction program just to give the business manager an idea of the type of instructions the programmer has to write. These COBOL instructions would then be punched up, entered into the computer, run against the COBOL translater program, and the actual machine code program would be generated. This program would probably be stored on a disc file to be called in and used when an inventory transaction program was run.

IBM — **COBOL PROGRAM SHEET**

System | Program | Programmer | Date | Punching Instructions: Graphic, Punch | Card Form # | * | Sheet of | Identification 73–80

Form No. X28-1464-2 U/M 050 Printed in U.S.A.

```
SEQUENCE  A   B
010 PROCEDURE DIVISION.
020 START.
030     OPEN I-O MASTERFILE, INPUT CARDFILE.
040 READ-CARD.
050     READ CARDFILE, AT END GO TO JOB-FINISHED.
060     MOVE ONECARD TO WORKAREA.
070
080 FIRST-STEP.
090     IF COLUMN-1 IS EQUAL TO 'W' GO TO WITHDRAWAL-ROUTINE.
100     IF COLUMN-1 IS EQUAL TO 'R' GO TO RECEIPT-ROUTINE.
110
120 WITHDRAWAL-ROUTINE.
130     MOVE PARTNUMBER TO MATCHAREA.
140     READ MASTERFILE.
150     DISPLAY MASTERCARD, 'BEFORE CHANGE/'.
160     SUBTRACT QUANTITY-ISSUED FROM ON-HAND.
170     DISPLAY MASTERCARD, 'AFTER CHANGE/'.
180     REWRITE MASTERCARD, AND GO TO READ-CARD.
190 RECEIPT-ROUTINE.
20      MOVE PARTNUMBER TO MATCHAREA.
21      READ MASTERFILE.
22      DISPLAY MASTERCARD, 'BEFORE CHANGE/'.
23      ADD QUANTITY-RECEIVED TO ON-HAND.
24      DISPLAY MASTERCARD, 'AFTER CHANGE/'.
25      REWRITE MASTERCARD AND GO TO READ-CARD.
```

* A standard card form, IBM electro C61897, is available for punching source statements from this form.

Figure 2

How does a computer process data then? Well, when all the mystery is dispelled, anyone who understands how people handle information has a pretty good idea of the way the computer will handle it. Consider another inventory application called "Material Requirements Planning," mentioned briefly in Chapter 2. This technique involves telling an inventory control man what the "Master Schedule" for the end product is. In other words, telling him how many of each end product will be made and when. His job is to use this master schedule to plan the "requirements" for material. To do this, he needs to have an inventory record and a bill of material (parts list).

He will plan the material requirements while looking at the master schedule for manufacturing the end product, checking the bill of material to see what sub-assemblies are needed in order to manufacture the end product, and then checking the inventory records for these sub-assemblies to see if they are on hand or on order. If insufficient quantities are on hand and on order, he will have to order enough of the sub-assemblies to make up the deficit. Before he can issue an order to make the sub-assemblies that are in short supply, he needs to know if parts are available to manufacture *them*. He then goes to the bill of material to find out what parts are required to make the particular sub-assemblies he needs. He then checks the inventory records for these parts. If some of the parts are not on hand or on order he will probably order more of them. If one of the machine parts requires raw material according to his bill of material, he will have to check to see if the raw material is available. If it is not on hand or on order he will have to order more of it.

The description above, of course, relates to a manual system. Computerized material requirements planning is one of the most common and profitable applications of the computer in a manufacturing company today — and it works exactly as described above. A master schedule is entered into the computer. The computer has two main files in it — one of them an inventory file and the other a bill of material file (usually called the "item master" file and "product structure file"). The computer checks the master schedule, checks the bill of material to see what parts are needed to make the end product, and it then goes to the inventory file to see if these parts are available. And just as the man did his requirements planning, the computer does material requirements planning. The main difference between the computerized system and the manual system is the ability of the computer to manipulate massive amounts of data rapidly and do a more responsive job of both planning requirements and replanning requirements as schedules are changed.

This brief description of the computer's capability then is intended to give the manager *confidence,* not necessarily *competence.* He doesn't really need competence in computer technology. He does need to understand the applications that go on the computer and to understand that basically the computer is doing the same things that were being done manually, only with a greatly advanced capability for manipulating data: Bringing information in, running it against files of information, and generating output information to tell people what action to take.

Too many operating managers still look at a computer much as a dog looks at a car: He accepts the fact that it can move forward or backward and if it suddenly moved straight up, he wouldn't be too surprised. The manager should understand that the computer is a technically complex machine, but its functions are quite simple.

Many managers are constantly asking their technicians "can I do _____ on my computer?" The technician can usually answer quite readily. If the information is in the files he can read it out. If he can input other information, and with the information in the files generate new information, he can give the manager the report he needs. It's sometimes pathetic to hear managers asking computer technical people whether or not they can get certain information when that information never existed in the first place and could not possibly be a product of the information that does exist. The rules are simple and they do not require genuises to understand them. It's incumbent upon every manager in business today to understand not only a few vital things about the computer, but to do his own thinking rather than relying 100 percent on the technicians to answer questions that should be obvious to anyone with even a rudimentary knowledge of the computer's capability. It isn't important to understand the theory of the internal combustion engine or the planetary transmission to drive an automobile. It certainly isn't necessary to understand very much about the computer to use it a great deal more intelligently than it has been used in the past.

WHERE ARE THE PAYOFFS?

When we first started using computers in business, it was a challenge to get the first application on the machine. The applications that were easiest were those that were most highly structured. Payroll is the application that most companies put on the computer right away. The logic behind the payroll computations is easy to capture and since the payroll system in most companies *did work* on a manual basis, putting it on the computer usually was not too challenging. On the other hand, this usually did not generate much in the way of benefits. Many companies, after putting payroll on the computer, found that while they might have eliminated some clerical help, the savings were usually more than offset by the cost of the computer, the programming staff, the systems people, etc.

Imaginative souls, seeing the vast potential capability and underestimating the difficulty of realizing this potential, quickly began to talk about developing "managing information systems." The idea, of course, was that by establishing all encompassing files of basic information ("the data base") management could be provided with all the information required to run the business properly. Vast sums of money have been spent on projects to develop management information systems, but somehow they never seem to get completed and never seem to generate results. Because everybody is talking about "management information systems" or "total information systems" a number of companies have decided that in order to be "advanced" and "sophisticated" they should support programs to develop management systems. To quote a later McKinsey report:[3]

> "Integrated total management information systems drawing on a single data base, which have so often been touted as the wave of the future, are another matter. They have not yet come to pass — and it is far from clear that they ever will."

McKinsey went on to say:

> "No company should embark on a program to develop a major management information system except to meet a specific, well-defined need."

To many companies this may sound like blasphemy, but the whole idea that the development of a management information system should be a top priority project is bunk — nonsense. The man who starts out to develop a management information system will probably never achieve anything. The man who starts out to solve specific company problems and in so doing tries to keep in mind how each new program could fit into an overall set of programs might someday have something resembling a management information system. But even that is highly dubious in the real world of ever-changing needs and people. There will always be considerable overlap and duplication in useful business oriented computer systems. The concept of the totally integrated systems does not seem to be compatible with the realities of the business world.

Progress takes place in a series of pendulum swings, from wild extremes like payroll to MIS with little to show for the effort. Today we are beginning to recognize that the payoff applications of the computer may not be terribly sophisticated; they

---

[3] *Unlocking the Computer's Profit Potential*, McKinsey & Company, Inc., 1968.

may not be totally integrated; but they are basically in areas where management needs more information, more pertinent information, more up-to-date information, or more rapid manipulation of information in order to make better decisions. In a manufacturing company the logistics part of its business — production and inventory management — is one of the most universal payoff applications. The reasons are not too difficult to understand; the crucial decisions made in "forecasting, manpower, and production scheduling and inventory management" have a tremendous impact on the success or failure of the business. They also require the manipulation of vast amounts of data on a timely basis.

Once again, however, it is necessary to sound a note of caution. It is easy to be enthused about the great potential applications for computers, but don't get razzle-dazzled by words. Many managers have been talked into believing a new dispatching system would give them better "control" over work in process and naturally assumed that this would enable them to reduce work-in-process inventory. Being able to assign better priorities and keep better track of the location of work in process doesn't really do anything to help reduce the overall *level* of work-in-process inventory. Anytime the manager doesn't clearly understand the "why" behind the anticipated results of the program that is being proposed, he should insist on a clearer explanation. He must be able to see the direct causal relationship between the new system that is going in and the results that are anticipated. It's easy to talk a good story and even many of the computer manuals themselves — often written by programming types who never have really worked in the factory (but are sure they understand all its problems) — frequently make some generous, false claims that can be very misleading to the uncritical manager.

Another good rule to go by is a very simple one:

If They Cannot Explain *Clearly* How and Why the Results Are Going to Happen to Your Satisfaction, They Probably Do Not Understand It Themselves.

One of the best ways to pick a payoff application area is to have someone who understands computers, computer systems, and the company's overall problems meet with the top manager as he sets objectives for his own managers. His objectives should be ambitious and demanding. A good systems man with his own knowledge of the company and his knowledge of what the computer can do should participate in trying to assist the manager in determining where the computer could best be used to improve the manager's own performance. The systems man should work from the point of view of solving the manager's problem, not from the point of view of the computer and all the great things that it can do. It's never a good idea to go to each manager and ask him "what he wants." If the manager doesn't understand modern computer applications he will easily revert to asking the systems man to computerize his manual system. This is often the worst possible way to waste the computer's capabilities! The important thing is to go to the managers and ask them what major problems they have in meeting their most important objectives. A good systems man should be able to determine how better information could help a manager to do his job better. The point is very simple:

Start from the Problem and Work to the Computer, Do Not Start from the Computer and Try to Apply Techniques that are Convenient for It to Handle.

Once managers see the computer as a tool to help them meet their objectives rather than as a technical tool that is being used by the specialists to play interesting games and generate large budget assessments, they begin to act more realistically about the computer. They realize that intelligent use of the computer is *their* responsibility, not something they can delegate to the technicians.

Picking the best applications to work on at any one time involves the same old difficult decisions we always faced in business. If a manager says he can get a particular result due to improved information from a new computer system, we have to ask the technical man "how" and "what" it will take in time and resources to get this computer system going. The investment can then be compared with the return in order to determine which projects should have the highest priority.

This is not always as simple as it sounds. There are some projects — like replacing an informal production and inventory control system with a formal one — that will produce most of the payoff through better control. And this is a difficult payoff to evaluate. It involves questions like "What is it worth to be able to respond to business increases faster and in a more organized manner?"

Only the manager can answer these questions. And this assumes that he understands modern computer applications to his business. He, not the systems man, is primarily responsible for understanding the applications. Undoubtedly he has only a limited knowledge of these applications, and he had better get a good understanding as quickly as he can. Sources for application education are discussed in Checklist 4.

It sounds familiar, doesn't it? The justification priority decisions are not easy and the responsibility for the decisions, as usual, rests with the manager. All this baloney we have heard about computers has only obscured a lot of the basic principles of business management that everyone should understand. Computers are just means to an end. They are ways to get the job done. The company that sets out with an objective of putting in a computer system is naive. The company that sets out to manage better and decides that computers are a valid modern tool that every manager should know how to use intelligently is most likely to get the real payoffs.

PAYOFFS IN PRODUCTION AND INVENTORY MANAGEMENT

The computer came along with its enhanced capability for manipulating data just about the time that the problems of production and inventory management were getting very difficult indeed. Increased pressure to provide greater customer service, increased pressure to keep inventories down, and the necessity for keeping people working at a more stable rate as well as keeping indirect costs in the factory under control have focused attention on production and inventory management. The fact that the computer promised to be of some help focused even more management attention on the area. To understand it better, let's review briefly some of the principal techniques.

Inventory management revolves around three major questions:

1. *What* should we exert our primary efforts on controlling?
2. *How much* should we reorder?
3. *When* should inventory reorders be placed?

The field of inventory management has long been aware of the basic concept of "ABC." This is merely an extension of the Pareto distribution — 20 percent of the items in inventory will account for 80 percent of the sales — to inventory management.

The second major question, how much to order, is dealt with by the *Economic Order Quantity* (EOQ) concept. Formulae for calculation have been around for some time and only very modest improvements on these calculations are possible with the computer. The economic order quantity concept has always tended to be misused. Most people felt that if they just calculated the economic order quantity they were doing the job. Actually, the calculations merely serve as a means to an end and show where profits can be obtained if someone goes after them. The ability to misuse this application has been somewhat enhanced by the computer because it is so easy to make the calculations. Variations on the economic order quantity concept, such as techniques for calculating order quantities when requirements are very sporadic, have been developed. In some cases, the computer can contribute to these calculations, and it can certainly contribute to the right kind of lot size analysis, but this is not one of its major contributions.

Calculating economic order quantities is a pre-planning function. In the day-to-day operation of an inventory control system, the really important question is the third one, "when." This is the part of the inventory system that determines the priorities that are used in the factory and that generates orders to vendors. The most commonly known reordering technique is the *order point.* This is a quantity that is pre-established so that when the inventory level gets down to this quantity, an order will be placed. The basic construction of the order point is very simple:

Order point = demand/lead time + safety stock

Consider an example where demand is forecast to be 100 units per week:

Lead time is estimated to be six weeks.

Theoretically, then, the material should be reordered when the inventory reaches a level of 600 units. Obviously, the forecast of demand is likely to be inaccurate. If sales don't meet the forecast, there will be some material on hand when the new supply comes in. If sales exceed the forecast, the supply of material will be exhausted before the new supply comes in. In order to protect against this contingency, order point systems practically always have some safety stock in them. Safety stock was classically a very rough estimate. Without going into details here, suffice it to say that safety stock is a function of the combined effects of

1. Forecast error.
2. The length and variability of the replenishment lead time.
3. The number of times material is reordered in a year (and thus runs the risk of having its supply exhausted).
4. The level of service needed.

The computer has made a real contribution to the calculation of more rational order points, since safety stocks can be calculated more effectively than they could with manual methods. Some statistical approximations can be used to measure forecast error, and techniques such as exponential smoothing (what a wild name for a technique that's really just an approximation to a moving average!) can be used to keep order points up-to-date. With manual systems, this was always a problem since there never seemed to be enough time to get the order points recalculated. The methods of applying these techniques of so-called "scientific inventory control" require enough computation so that the computer is a real boon to people who have items in inventory that require order point type control.

The other basic method for determining when to reorder is material requirements planning. This technique was explained briefly in the previous chapter. Rather than reorder an inventory item when it gets down to a predetermined level or order point, inventory items that are controlled by requirements planning are reordered to cover anticipated future requirements. These requirements are calculated by estimating how many of the end product or assembly will be built and by calculating *what* requirements will be needed *when*. Both are arrived at by entering a master schedule and having it generate requirements for the assemblies. The computer then checks the inventory availability for each assembly. When there are not enough to cover requirements, it goes to the bill of material file to find out what parts are required.

Requirements planning has proven to be an even more significant payoff application than statistical order point calculations because of the massive amounts of data to be manipulated. As schedules change, it is desirable in an inventory system to go to the bill of material file and recalculate the requirements for all parts. With a manual system, this simply is not practical. With a computer system it is.

What is the state of the art today in computerized inventory management? Actually, it's pretty sad. Practically anyone who was making a forecast five years ago would have estimated that far more progress would have been made by today, but several problems have presented themselves:

1. Because order point techniques have received far more publicity than requirements planning techniques, they were often misapplied. Order points apply primarily to finished goods, items, or repair parts that are no longer used in current production. Requirements planning is the preferable technique for any components that go into assemblies, semi-finished items, repair parts that are used in current production, and in any other situation where demand is "dependent." *Dependent demand* simply means that the item cannot be looked at in inventory by itself. It should not be reordered independently since its demands come from other items that are also in inventory and can best be calculated based on plans for manufacturing those items, rather than average demand for the item itself. For example, a component that goes into an assembled product might be withdrawn from inventory in a sufficient quantity to make six month's supply of the assembled product. If the component is immediately reordered, it is likely to get into inventory long before it is needed. On the other hand, if it is used in two or three different items, the demand could be very low for a period of time and no reorders created, then suddenly all of the assemblies using it might create demands. Far better to use requirements planning here than an order point system that bases inventory levels on past usage.

    The principle of independent/dependent demand was developed in 1965 by Dr. J. A. Orlicky, Manufacturing Industry Consultant for IBM, in order to provide a guide for people in knowing where and where not to apply order points versus material requirements planning. Even today, however, some people are not aware of the principles, and, since requirements planning only became a practical technique with the computer, it is often relatively poorly understood by many practitioners.

2. Another serious problem was the fad for sophistication that was so characteristic of the 1960's. Anything that didn't involve complex mathematical calculations was considered to be rather mundane and hardly worthy of the attention of real intellectual types, who generally were those who were working around the computer. As a result, when statistical order point was installed, it was usually installed in a highly mathematical fashion that was unintelligible to the users. Requirements planning was largely overlooked because it only involved massive data manipulation without a lot of sophisticated mathematics. It was looked upon as a rather pedestrian computer application. Once again, the sophistication mania took its toll.

3. All of the other classical reasons for systems failure applied to inventory systems. Too often, the systems man himself designed the system, and he usually assumed that the computer rather than the people was going to control the inventory, and too often the system was implemented "cold turkey."

   One of the biggest problems that existed in trying to get better inventory control systems on the air was, quite simply, the fact that many companies were not yet ready to manage with a system. They failed to see the significance of accurate inventory records, accurate records for bills of material, and realistic master schedules. They tended to look on systems as something rather mysterious, with unfathomable logic, rather than as practical, simple management tools. As a result, very few of them ever worked.

In day-to-day operation, a production and inventory control system is concerned with four fundamental functions:

1. Planning priorities.
2. Planning capacities.
3. Controlling capacities.
4. Controlling priorities.

The inventory system is primarily concerned with the "when" question — planning of priorities. It is from the inventory system that capacity plans need to be developed, since if we do not know what material is needed, it is rather hard to develop the factory capacity requirements to manufacture that material. Controlling priorities usually involves some form of shop floor control, where a dispatch list is often generated from the computer — usually on a daily basis — to let the factory floor know what the latest job priorities are.

This is not a book on production and inventory control so the details of modern approaches to capacity planning and control and priority control will not be discussed. Suffice it to say that the computer has made a dramatic impact in these areas, once again because of its great ability to manipulate data. For our purposes, since we are going to use material requirements planning as an example throughout the balance of this book, it is important to recognize how it fits into a system and to recognize how important it is that it be developed first. This assumes, of course, that the company has, as most companies do have, dependent demand inventory items.

WILL THE REAL SYSTEM PLEASE STAND UP?

In Chapter 1, we discussed the fact that most companies operate with an informal system rather than a formal system. In complex areas such as the logistics end of the business, this is particularly true since in the past formal systems couldn't possibly do the job. Let's think, for example, about the objectives of an inventory system. It is rather apparent that an inventory control system should

1. Order material.
2. Order the material with the right priority on it.
3. Maintain the right priority on the material after the order has been released.

Whenever the order point system is being used incorrectly for the control of dependent demand components, you can be sure that only luck will put the right due dates on any components. This can be verified in the shop or in the purchasing department, where many inventory replenishment orders are late and no one is expediting them (because the informal system recognizes that they are not needed at the moment and that other items — some of them with far later delivery dates — are actually needed immediately to meet requirements on the assembly floor). So the order point system, when used incorrectly on dependent demand items only meets objective number 1. It tends to have a great deal of material on order, occasionally it does not have material on order when it is needed, but for the most part *everything* tends to be on order with a large percentage of the items late and not actually needed. The order point system certainly cannot meet objective number 2 or objective number 3 for dependent demand items.

Manual or punched-card requirements planning systems are really only a little bit better. They tend to order material with the right due date, but because of their inability to recalculate due dates as requirements change, they cannot meet objective number 3. Consider, for example, the situation where a casting is scrapped in process. New castings are ordered but at best they will not be in for eight weeks in spite of all the expediting effort that has been exerted. At this point, all other parts that go into the assembly using the casting should be rescheduled. Many inventory control people of the old school will not agree with this. Their general approach to life is "a bird in the hand is worth two in the bush," but, of course, this is partly because they have lived in the era of informal systems. Whenever the boss came around and asked them where something was or why there was a parts shortage, they could always point to the fact that they had ordered the material and that it was late — this was easy since their inventory system usually arranged to have *everything late!* Only the expediting system could tell which items were really needed — and always too late. Actually, when one part is not going to be available to make an assembly, the other parts should be rescheduled since, if shop capacity or vendor capacity is reasonably well adjusted to the level required, anytime you make some things you do not need, the chances are extremely good that the factory or vendors will not be making things that are needed. More important than that, any system that puts false dates on parts tends to break down. One of the most dependable rules of systems is

The Truth Will Out!

Imagine a foreman working on some parts because the date on the order says they must be done by next week. The foreman of the assembly department comes in to the first foreman's department and asks him why he's working on these parts when some other parts are actually holding up an assembly at the present moment. In a very short period of time, these two foremen will realize that they can find out what parts are needed by getting together once a day with a shortage list — and do it better than the formal system will!

In the past, inventory systems in a complex business simply were not capable of meeting all three objectives of an inventory system. In fact, in most companies, you could see two systems in operation — one a "push" system, the inventory system generating orders, and the other a "pull" system. The pull system was the expediters and the foremen down on the shop floor who really kept the priorities up-to-date. The foreman would tell an expediter what parts he needed in order to meet the assembly schedule, and the expediter would have these parts pulled ahead of time in the storeroom and make up a shortage list which he would give to another foreman in the sub-assembly department. He would then convey the other information to his expediters, and this informal system would practically do the entire job of getting parts through. Usually necessitating a tremendous amount of effort, and only being able to detect parts shortages at the last moment so that excessive expediting and all its attendant inefficiencies result. (It is

interesting to observe in most companies how much time a foreman spends expediting when very few foremen have this in their
job description.) Very few managers see the big picture well
enough to recognize how much informal systems in the logistics
area are the cause of poor quality, of personnel problems, of excessive downtime resulting from poor supervision, and of all the
other evils that result when a foreman is not managing his department well, simply because he does not have the time to do it
because he must work hard at the informal system if he is to
produce for one more day.

Material requirements planning on a computer does have the
capability, and this has been proven a number of times in many
types of businesses, to meet all three objectives of an inventory
system. As was mentioned above, it is also the necessary pre-
requisite to a good capacity planning system, and certainly to a
good shop floor control system, because one of the most important objectives of shop floor control is to communicate the
proper priorities to the shop floor. For this reason, in the balance
of the book, material requirements planning will be used as an
example of a system being designed and installed. This certainly
does not mean that it is the only system, or even that it is the
most important system in *all* companies, but it is a widely applicable system in manufacturing companies and can serve as a practical reference to illustrate many points to be made.

IS IT REALLY GOING TO PAY OFF?

The potential improvements possible from the installation of a
material requirements planning system on the computer are substantial. Because it can replace the informal system, it is possible
to get very substantial results from improved management by foremen and by people in production control, who can spend less of
their time firefighting and more time planning. It is also possible

to get better performance out of purchasing. They cannot expedite everything, and, when a large percentage of all items are late, they can always be the scapegoats. At the same time purchasing can always come up with an excuse for not performing to the priorities set by the inventory system. With the right kind of inventory system, they can be given a plan that they can meet, and, as a consequence, they can be held responsible for meeting the plan. With less need for expediting, purchasers can spend more time on buying and do a better job of controlling and reducing purchased material costs.

These are the intangibles. Most companies are not likely to realize a great deal from intangibles because they do not recognize that they should get these kinds of benefits. They do not set better objectives for people as a result of the improved system and they do not follow up to see that they have achieved them. Nevertheless, the intangibles are there. A truly efficient manager *can* get these kinds of results from better inventory systems.

There are real tangible results, and these are the ones that should be used to justify the system if a new computer is to be installed. Material requirements planning on a computer, when properly designed and implemented, can give the following results:

1. Component inventories reduced from 20 to 50 percent.
2. Customer service improved substantially. Some users have had a 90 percent reduction in late orders shipped to customers.
3. Reduced manufacturing costs — up to 10 percent less spent on assembly labor (because all of the parts are available to make the product more frequently, and it is not necessary to partially build things or put them aside). Up to 5 percent greater productivity overall (due to less expediting, having to break into set-ups, etc.).
4. Fewer indirect employees — up to 25 percent fewer storekeepers, expediters, truckers, and clerks (most people don't get a 25 percent reduction in cost, however, since they

usually upgrade the requirements and pay of these people).[4]

How do you know these things can be done in your company? Obviously, you do not, but you can make some conservative estimates, and, since informal systems are usually so inefficient, even if you have to justify a computer it is not too difficult in any complex manufacturing business to justify a computer on material requirements planning alone.

Here, however, we are up against a classical situation. The potential is so obvious that the manager can easily believe that it can happen without doing the things that are necessary to make it happen. Putting a computer system in will not automatically do it, and when the system is being justified he should be sure to assign the responsibility for results to the responsible managers and not to systems people. *Never approve a systems proposal where the justification was provided by systems people, outside consultants, or representatives of the hardware manufacturers.*

The responsible manager must sign his name and must agree that the system can give him the information to generate the results to justify the system. If he does not feel that it can, either he does not understand or the system is one more wild dream. The important thing to recognize is that even if the system has the potential for providing the results, unless he is going to make it happen, it will not. There is no such thing as a system that will generate results. *The computer is only a means for implementing a system; the system is a means for providing information; systematic information can be used by managers to get better results.*

How do you know that the results claimed are possible? One of the best ways is to talk to other people who have done similar things. This is becoming more and more practical. Companies are not all that different. If the companies make an assembled product, they probably have a lot of the same kinds of inventory

---

[4] This information was drawn from the American Production and Inventory Control Society Special Report No. 2, Washington, D.C., 1971.

problems. If they have branch warehouses, they probably share a great many similar problems. The manager should be *sure* that *he* can get these results before approving a systems proposal.

Justification in the past often involved bringing in a new computer, frequently the first one. Justification for a system today is usually based on getting time on the present computer or buying additional computer services. Frequently the company cannot afford to make the financial investment at the present time to add to its computer capacity. *It's important then, that the new system be justified in relation to the other systems.*

What this means very simply is that people tend to look at the new system and ask whether it can justify another computer, for example. This is certainly not the correct way to do it. The real question is whether the new system should displace some of the current systems (like the bowling averages, golf handicaps, and miscellaneous accounting records that could be done by a clerk with a comptometer) that are already in the computer.

The computer is very much like the average woman's refrigerator. Within a very short time after it appears on the scene, it's full — and most of what is in it is junk. When a new computer comes into a company, everybody struggles valiantly to get its "utilization" as high as possible. The result is that when a real payoff application comes along, there usually is not enough computer time to handle it. The manager who really wants to use the computer to make money in his business should have enough plain guts to tell people to take some of their applications off the computer and either to do them manually or have them done at an outside service bureau and have the department that needs the information pay the cost.

Most companies have a number of time-consuming programs that run up many computer hours. One that I know of runs thirteen labor distribution reports — only three of these are even sent to factory management personnel. The question of what can be eliminated, combined, or run less frequently is a tough one to answer. Here is where a real management-oriented systems man could help, since most users of reports cannot see the "big picture" and know where duplication and extra expense are being incurred. By the same token, the data processing people usually have no way to evaluate the relative importance of these reports.

Before more computer power is purchased a good manager will insist that all present reports be reviewed. The computer is a precious resource.

THE WHEEL DOES NOT NEED MORE DEVELOPMENT WORK

Back when companies were first developing more systematic approaches to controlling their business, many managers visited companies that were reputed to be doing a good job of putting in better systems. The first temptation was to "lift" the system that one company used successfully and put it in another. This is very much like going from one patient to another in the hospital to find out what the doctor prescribed to cure him. The fact that one cure happened to work for one particular disease doesn't necessarily mean that it will work for another disease. People rapidly learned that they could not pick up a system from one company, install it in another company, and get good results.

At that point companies began to design their own systems to solve their own problems. We then entered the age of the custom-made system. Yet if one goes from company to company it is pretty obvious that the problems are not all that different. One company may have a particular variation of the problem, but it certainly does not need a completely customized system to solve problems that are not completely unique.

Today we are beginning to look upon systems as groups of standard techniques that can be used to solve similar problems. The system itself needs to be customized for the individual company much as a man's suit needs to be tailored to fit him. The company that starts out to develop its own system from scratch too frequently emulates the man who decides that he can economically design his own wearing apparel without drawing upon the experience of others. What he comes up with may be unique, but it probably will not be very utilitarian, and certainly the return on investment will be very low indeed. Before the manager decides to go ahead with an appropriation for any system, he should be sure that it embodies fairly standard techniques unless he is completely convinced that he has a really unique problem.

There are several factors that motivate people to develop unique solutions to standard problems:

1. The NIH factor (*Not Invented Here*). If it wasn't developed by us it is no good. This is a normal kind of problem that management should always be aware of and try to direct people away from. Too often the senior managers themselves have a good dose of NIH — especially if the system involved was developed at *another division* of their company.

2. Many systems people believe the nonsense that so many pandering magazine articles and speakers throw at them. They fancy themselves "designers" and feel that they can "do it better." Like the misguided engineer who blows his ego designing custom nuts and bolts, this type of systems man is a real, and not uncommon, liability.

3. "Our company is different" is a common phrase in any business enterprise. "We make wire and cable, our problems are different!" There are differences, of course, but companies fit into a very limited number of general categories. Most of the logistics problems of companies manufacturing assembled products, for example, are practically identical. It is a source of great pride to claim that "our company is different." It is also an excuse for not making progress, and an excuse for inventing new and expensive solutions to common problems.

On the other hand, there are many reasons why standard approaches *are* more satisfactory for most companies:

1. They are easier to develop since there is less time required to "design" them. There are many sound application programs available today that require only tailoring or customizing to fit a particular company's needs. These can be great time savers.

2. It is easier to train people since they can see this type of system in operation in other companies. Often "canned" training packages are available.

3. People using standard approaches can better communicate with and learn from others. Standard approaches are an essential element in multi-division corporation systems if they are to be successful and reasonably economical.

4. As the problems of people mobility become more and more prevalent, standard approaches are more and more essential. When a man who designed and installed his own original system leaves a company they can be in real trouble.

5. Standard systems tend to be more desirable because they do not have the stamp of one man on them, and as managers change they tend to see them as standard tools rather than insisting on developing their own unique approaches.

6. Standard approaches tend to get people off the "his" and "mine" preoccupation. This gets them out of a *design* and into a *results* mode much quicker.

The hard-headed businessman should insist that he be shown similar techniques working in other companies that are similar — but certainly not identical — from a control point of view. He probably will not see too many companies that make exactly the same product in the same way he does. He should, however, see companies that do have the same problems of controlling branch warehouse inventories, for example, or getting all the parts together to make an assembled product, or planning capacities well enough so that the plant does not always have to run behind schedule, etc.

This requires then, a high degree of plain good business judgment. This involves the ability to discriminate between systems approaches that will work in one company but will not work in another because the problems are entirely different, while recognizing that problems in each company tend to be similar and that the systems to solve these problems need to be tailored, not designed from the gound up.

THE PROPOSAL

When the manager is satisfied that he has a potentially profitable computer application, he will probably want to have a proposal made to request resources for systems development and implementation. These proposals are often made by systems people or users who are very close to their own problems. Here are some guidelines to follow in making proposals:

1. Make them brief. Detail belongs in an appendix. Top management should not be expected to read a mass of technical trivia.
2. Avoid jargon and sophistication for its own sake. This is "show off" stuff and has no place in a management proposal. Two points are deducted each time an acronym or the word "parameter" is used.
3. Make sure the objectives and performance measures are identified.
4. The users must sign off on the results to be attained.
5. Make sure these objectives are ambitious. Most successful systems could be used to generate even better results than they do.

SYSTEMS AS A MEANS TO AN END

Having a computer available to handle systems such as material requirements planning has enabled some companies to largely eliminate their informal systems. As a result, they have much more
responsive systems that free people to do the kind of work that
people really do best. There is no need to have people trying to figure
out what parts are really needed when they should be spending their
time trying to figure out much more complex problems that
computers simply are not adapted to. For example, how to motivate
people to get the most productivity out of them, how to manage
people to avoid the mutually crippling effects of a strike, and what
can be done to train operators to avoid the quality problems that
mathematical techniques such as statistical quality control can
detect but not cure. The main job is managing. The big benefit of the
computer is that it can free people from the drudgery of manipulating data and enable them to do their jobs better. This is
especially true since people cannot really do the kinds of things that
computers can do. No human being could calculate the changing
requirements for 30,000 to 40,000 manufactured and purchased
parts on a regular basis. For a computer this job is easy and, in fact,
one of the best possible tests of a potential computer application is
simply this:

Why Do Anything On a Computer
That You Can Do Manually?

There is nothing inherently wrong with doing some things on
a computer that can be done manually. But the important thing is
to do those things on a computer that *couldn't possibly* be done
manually. The rescheduling of 30,000 to 40,000 parts, the
planning of capacity, the recalculation of priorities, keeping up to
date on the branch warehouse needs so we can distribute inven-

tory most effectively. These are kinds of applications that really payoff.

The value of the computer based system is not so much in reducing numbers of people but in gaining real control and freeing many people from the necessity of spending the bulk of their working hours struggling to do a job that cannot be done well without a formal system. When a successful computer based system is implemented, it probably will not reduce the hours managers work. But it can enhance their capability to manage, by freeing them from less important tasks dictated by the informal system's requirements, and by giving them better information to manage with.

What the managers must understand is that systems — in spite of the claims of overzealous systems people — won't control business. Only people can do that. The manager must insist that the "fog" and baloney be dispersed so that he can understand the new techniques that are possible with the computer. Because he — and only he — is responsible for getting results from the system.

4

Organizing the Systems Team

"We have met the enemy and he is us."
                                        Pogo

HOW TO DO IT DEAD WRONG

There is a tried and proven formula for making computer systems fail. It usually works something like this:

1. Hire a man from outside to take the job of systems/data processing manager. Obviously none of your people have the potential. Be sure that he is the technical type who has a high disdain for people on the firing line, like foremen, salesmen, machine operators, and the like.

2. Have him report to the president. Obviously his efforts must cross departmental lines and he has to have the kind

of support to enable him to impose his system in spite of other people's objections.

3. Encourage him to staff with the most highly trained people he can get. Preferably, M.B.A.'s from some of the better-known colleges who have very strong management science backgrounds.

4. Hire a consultant. Preferably one that is big, well-known, and can supply you with four or five resident consultants for a few years to take the burden of developing this system off the hands of your people. Don't bother to get any references on the individual resident consultants who are supposed to do the job for you. You have the word of this reputable consulting firm that these people are competent. *Obviously,* the consulting firm will have to put in a successful system since their reputation depends on it.

5. Start out to develop a total management information system. Give it an acronym — how about TOMIS?[1]

Let us analyze a few of the reasons for this approach being consistently dead wrong.

If you are going to hire a man to head up your computer effort, judge him first on his management ability and second on his technical ability. Be sure that he understands that systems don't run businesses, people do. And be sure that he is, above all, a good salesman. Where he reports in the organization is not as important as who he reports to. His superior should be objective enough to want to see the computer used where it can really generate profitable results. He should also be aggressive enough to insist that profitable applications get developed.

The coordination across departmental lines is a selling job, not one that can be imposed no matter what level the man reports to. No system is so good that it will work in spite of the lack of reception the users give to it.

---

[1] I thought this one up myself; but I'll bet someone, someplace is already using it! To him my sincere apologies. Also my best wishes for a great deal of luck.

Chapter 2 dealt with the problem of sophistication. The more sophisticated technical types you get on a design team, the more they will tend to invent their own wheel rather than use things that have already been developed. It would be unrealistic to expect many men who have spent most of their school hours studying highly sophisticated mathematical solutions to problems to be capable of developing simple solutions to the basic problems that beset the typical company today. It may be necessary to hire someone from outside, but the bulk of the job should be done by your own people who understand your company and your product — and are not likely to leave to go to the next company that offers a $1500 a year salary increase. Investing your money in training your own people will pay greater rewards than hiring a number of technical "professionals."

Most consultants are in the business of renting bodies. It simply is not economically feasible to have very highly paid people operating at the resident consulting level. This means that the resident consultant is generally one of three types:

1. A young man recently out of college who does not know very much about business except what he has learned from books. If he has any experience, it is probably in systems or data processing.
2. A man who has not been successful in his career and has turned to consulting as the last resort. This type is usually not very good at handling people and has seldom witnessed a successful system. His confidence comes from his general belief that, having witnessed so many failures, he knows what is right by the process of elimination.
3. Occasionally a dedicated man with a high professional interest is willing to put up with the long hours, unreasonable travel requirements and modest salary given to a resident consultant in order to further his own career. These men are the exceptions, not the rule.

One of the most difficult problems in getting a new system

operating is getting the users to accept the responsibility for generating results from the system. The more systems people you have in the act and the more outside consultants you have available to shift the responsibility to, the less the users are likely to accept the responsibility for results.

Many companies have a false sense of security about hiring a consultant. They feel that the consultant has a reputation to protect and obviously cannot afford to fail. This is poppycock! Ask any reputable consultant, and he will give you the names of three or four disreputable consultants who have been in business for years. Behind them they have a long unbroken string of failures with only a few rare instances where anything that they have proposed has worked. How do they continue in business? Most of them operate on the very sound premise of P. T. Barnum: "There is one born every minute."

Very few companies ever check the credentials of people who are actually going to do the job for them, and most of them don't realize that consulting contracts are really worthless. They are intended primarily to protect the consultant, not the client. If a consultant works on a system and it is not successful, he can almost always point to the people who are supposed to use this system and claim that they did not cooperate and were not of a high enough caliber to understand the system. There is just enough truth to this statement to make it impossible for the client to refute it in spite of the vast amounts of money he may have spent for scant success.

One other aspect of human nature that helps even the most disreputable consulting firm is people's reluctance to admit that they have been duped. In Chapter 2 the example of one of the most reputable consulting firms in the country that sent in a number of M.B.A.'s to develop a highly sophisticated control system was mentioned. It cost $250,000 and did not work. All the vice president who hired the consultant had as a result was a number of binders with reams and reams of paper, formulae and explanations. Nevertheless, he was publicly enthusiastic about the job that had been done, although he privately confided that it had been a total failure. But he could not possibly admit this without jeopardizing his own position within his company for having been so foolish! Some consultants flourish for the same reason that con men flourish.

There is one other aspect of consulting that is particularly interesting to think about. Auditing firms today almost always have a "Management Services" group. During their auditing activities these firms may criticize some of their client companies' practices. Obviously, the first question that a responsible management is likely to ask is where they can get help to correct these practices. The "Management Services" provided by the auditing firm seems a rather obvious answer.

It would seem that this group above all cannot afford to put in an unsuccessful system for their client. Unfortunately, the record shows a different picture entirely. Auditing firms have been among the most unsuccessful in keeping up with modern techniques in the area of manufacturing control. They can use the standard excuses of the consultant, and there is considerable evidence to indicate that they have an even greater ability to survive a poor consulting job than the regular management consultant.

This is not to say that auditing firms cannot do good consulting work or that you should never have an M.B.A. working for you on a consulting job. The intent is to point out that there is *no way* for a company to delegate responsibility for results to an outsider. The company that is naive enough to believe that they can sit back and let the consultant do the job for them without having to get their own hands dirty has not a chance of having a successful computer system. In this day of increasing technology we need consultants. We need to draw on specialized knowledge. The company that refuses to use consultants in any way is as foolish as the company that tries to sub-contract its management to a consulting firm. But no system will manage the business, and consultants cannot sell muscles, only coaching.

THE MYTH OF THE SYSTEMS SUPERMAN

Before we had computers we had systems people. They generally designed forms to improve the flow of paperwork and helped us to make our approaches to business more systematic. There were not too many of them around before the days of the computer, but there were a few.

With the advent of the computer, the need for systems people became obvious. There were programmers who talked to the computer and managers who needed to use the computer to be able to do their jobs better. Unfortunately, when the manager sits down to talk to the computer programmer, he finds himself in a very frustrating situation talking to a man who does not understand *his* job anymore than *he* understands the programmer's job. We need systems people who can talk both to the computer programmer and to the manager. Unquestionably, this is a valid concept, but like any other valid concept, it does not take very long to get distorted in practice.

Today, too many systems people think of themselves as systems "designers" — people who understand all aspects of business and also understand the computer. They are usually quite critical of many of the approaches being used by business people. In spite of the fact that they have never handled any of these positions of responsibility themselves, they feel quite confident that they understand "how it should be done."

The problem, of course, is very simple. Their knowledge of these functions is often superficial and generally was taken from computer manuals. Computer manuals are almost always written by systems people who were once programmers and who have had a couple of plant tours and talked with a few data processing people about their problems. Armed with a strong confidence in their general ability, they write manuals which are mainly intended to help market computers and computer programs. Too many systems people read these manuals, believe them, and believe that, having read them, they really understand what the problems and solutions are. When they go out and talk to the people who really have the problems and try to show them how better systems could help, their natural reaction is often to assume that these people are pretty ignorant because they do not react enthusiastically.

The systems man may often understand some new techniques better than the manager does, and he may often understand how these techniques can be applied using a computer, but his job is to *sell new ideas to the manager* and to avoid trying to design the systems himself. He should not try to create the reaction; he should be the catalyst that makes the reaction happen at a much faster rate.

This is not to say that we do not need systems people, nor is it to say that there are not a number of dedicated, practical, down-to-earth, profit-oriented systems people around in spite of the cult of sophistication. But the minute a systems man takes the design initiative, he insulates the user from the computer and perpetuates the myth of the magic machine. He also relieves the user of responsibility for getting the kinds of systems that he thinks are needed. He also runs the risk of introducing simplistic ideas. It is easy for a systems man to get himself in real trouble by asking users questions like "Shouldn't we always release the oldest order first in the order entry system?" The user will almost always agree with this type of question without thinking about the fact that there are times when the president wants an order to go ahead of all other orders. Or that the sales manager often insists on special service to a customer who is threatening to stop doing business with the company. Or that there is a large customer who does a good job of measuring his vendors' performance and will make life miserable if his order is not shipped on time. These are the realities of the business world. Often the user himself does not like to think about them. The systems man who designs the system to ignore them is in for real trouble.

This may sound like an indictment of systems people; it is not intended to be. They have been exposed to a lot of baloney. The vast propaganda machine of the "Operations Research-Systems/Data Processing-Consulting-Academia" establishment is constantly bombarding them with sophisticated nonsense. Just sample the articles, computer manuals, and technical society talks and meetings. The man with the latest sophisticated hardware is the group hero, the fair-haired boy of the hardware salesmen and the envy of his peers. One could soon begin to believe that having an "on-line, real-time system" was the ultimate business objective. That great word *sophisticated* is in continual use; it always means *good!*

The wonder is that so many systems and data processing people have been able to keep some semblance of practical business orientation in this mad world! Within many companies the systems people are the bright ray of hope on the horizon. They are the people who want to make things better. They are the people who see the computer as a tool that management can use to run businesses more successfully. While the users are busily fighting fires, the systems people are urging that new and better approaches be taken.

But somehow the role of the systems man in many companies has become distorted. He has seen users who are all too willing to pass the buck to him to get the system developed. He has recognized that if he did not do the developing nothing would happen. Too often he has jumped in and assumed the responsibility for getting the system developed, and therefore, also tacitly assumed the responsibility for getting good results from a system. Often systems people are blinded by the sheer beauty and logic of their systems so that they fail to recognize — at least temporarily — that no system is so good that it will work if people do not want it to work. And that few systems are so good that the user will really try to make them work if he has not spilled some of his own blood and invested some of his own time in the development of the system. He must have a proprietary feeling if the system is to be successful. Many a major fiasco has started the day the systems people said "Well, it is obvious that they are not going to take the time to do the job, so we had better just design it ourselves." Advice to systems people: *If the users will not get involved do not — under any circumstances — take the initiative.*

THE CASE OF THE UNINVOLVED MANAGER

Many operating managers are too busy drowning to save themselves. They have day-to-day problems that are very serious, and while they would like to see some solutions to these problems, in many cases they have contented themselves by explaining away the problems as being the fault of someone else. In many companies, for example, the sales department blames the poor service on the manufacturing department. The manufacturing department blames the inability to make a profitable showing in the factory on the sales department. The engineering department is very critical of both departments and blames its failures on either unrealistic demands and too short a timetable for implementing them from the sales department, or inability of the manufacturing department to follow their instructions. The manufacturing department, of course, can point to the fact that the engineering group seldom gives them a completed design and practically never stops designing the product, even while it is in the middle of being manufactured. These are not unusual problems. When managers decide that they do not need to improve their functions because the only problem with their function is the difficulties created by unreasonable people on the outside, they are not mature enough to be entrusted with the responsibility of running a business.

Managers also have frequently had poor experiences with computer applications. Often some systems man has come along with rosy stories about the wonderful things that were going to happen when the computer was installed. The manager sat back and waited for the miracle, and of course, it never happened.

Instead of blaming himself for not having participated in the program and directed it so that it could give him better tools to work with, he blames the systems people and scoffs at the computer, vowing never again to get embroiled in another computer "mess."

Often the systems man has had a very frustrating experience when he went to the managers and asked them "What do you need" from the computer. Unfortunately, managers are not typically capable of answering this question very intelligently. Most of their experience has been with non-computer oriented systems. They are as unlikely to come up with a realistic answer about what their information needs are as a ditch digger is to describe a steam shovel if someone asks him what he needs. But if the manager intends to survive and thrive in a world where computers are going to be part of our everyday business life from now on, he had better learn very quickly what the computer can do for him in his job. The user then should understand the following points:

1. In many facets of business today there are better ways to do it. The computer can be of assistance in giving the manager better and more timely information to handle this function.

2. Responsibility for developing these better ways rests with the man who has the responsibility for the function, not with the systems people.

3. Systems people can generate ideas, assist in implementing these ideas, and in general help the manager to get what he wants. The essential responsibility for determining *what* he wants rests with the user.

4. *The responsibility for systems success must be assigned to the user.*

THE SYSTEMS DESIGN TEAM

Let us assume that we have a company that is organized along fairly conventional lines. There is a president, or if it is a division of a larger corporation, a general manager. He has reporting to him a plant manager who has the responsibility for industrial engineering, quality control, production and inventory control, etc. He also has an executive in charge of design and/or sales engineering, a financial executive, etc. The financial executive in our example will have the responsibility for the computer. He will have a data processing manager reporting to him and a systems manager. This is not to say that this is an ideal organizational arrangement, but it is a fairly typical one.

At least once a year — and hopefully more often — the general manager sits down with his people and discusses objectives for the coming year. Let us assume that his major objectives, passed down to his plant manager, include:

1. An improvement in customer service.
2. A reduction in inventory.
3. A reduction in material cost.
4. A reduction in scrap.

The plant manager and the general manager discuss the objectives they are shooting for, while the systems man is sitting in on their discussions. The systems man points out that the current inventory system is unresponsive and that he has heard of more effective inventory systems that can be employed using the computer. He suggests that the improved inventory systems could help to give a better customer service inventory level relationship. They discuss this further with the purchasing agent, who indicates that an inventory system that could better project anticipated requirements would give him an opportunity to negotiate more favorable terms and reduce purchased material costs. He also points out that a system which could better anticipate and update changes in material requirement dates could help him to reduce expediting cost and allow his people to spend more time expediting things that are really needed rather than a great many items that are late but often not really needed.

The plant manager further suggests that if he had more up-to-date scrap reporting information, rather than the once a month reports that he now gets two weeks after the close of the month, he could take corrective action to reduce scrap by 20 percent. This is verified with the quality control manager who agrees and suggests a particular format for the scrap reports. The systems man agrees that this kind of report can be developed independently of the proposed revised inventory system and that it can be developed quickly and with a minimum of expenditure.

The plant manager insists that one of the foremen be the chairman of the committee for redesigning the scrap reports. Also on the committee will be the quality control manager and the systems man. The ultimate responsibility for the new report will rest with this foreman, and as the system is designed, the rest of the foremen and the general foremen will be kept up to date on the new proposed system with particular emphasis on the role that they must play in achieving results with the system.

The plant manager now goes to his production and inventory control manager and discusses the objectives for improved performance in the area of customer service, inventory, and material costs for the coming year. He also points out that the systems man has suggested that an improved inventory system would provide better tools to make it more possible to achieve these objectives. The production and inventory control man is unenthusiastic. This is not particularly surprising, since he is not familiar with computer systems and has probably heard many tales of disaster from other companies that have tried to computerize their production and inventory control. He is justifiably skeptical.

At this juncture both the production and inventory control manager and the systems man, as well as the plant manager, should learn something more about the computer applications in production and inventory control. Perhaps this means going to one of the short classes conducted by consultants, the American Management Association, or one of the computer manufacturers. There are disadvantages with all three. Most consultants running educational programs are also promoting their own consulting services. Most computer manufacturers running educational programs have computer salesmen as instructors. To them anything done on a computer is good and anything not done on a computer is bad. Seminars put on by the American Management Association or other professional groups tend to be a series of loosely related speakers rather than genuine education. They are good for initial exposure but certainly do not represent structured, integrated, well-organized educational programs. When there is nothing else available, as is the case in so many fields today, these programs are better than nothing. Very few of the universities have anything of value that could be helpful at this juncture. A few of them have tried to develop continuing education programs with varying degrees of success. In fact, it is a rather sad commentary that the kind of education that the people in our hypothetical example would require is generally available only at a very low quality level. Most courses are either a series of loosely related individual talks or they have commercial overtones of one type or another. The company should look for the very best education available from the most professional, objective source possible.

Let us assume that the production control manager, having been exposed to some of the things that can be done by computers in production and inventory control, is cautiously interested. The computer salesman is now called in. He recommends some plant visitations to other companies using similar systems. He discusses some of the computer application programs that his company has that might be useful. After visiting some other plants, the production and inventory control manager agrees that he might be able to attain the goals being set for him if a system could be developed. The production and inventory control man's normal reaction at this point may be to go back to business as usual and wait for the systems man to develop something for him. Or perhaps they will call in a consulting firm and tell the consulting firm to develop the system for them. Neither approach is sound.

Who will take charge of this project? The plant manager should insist that the production control manager now free up his most valuable man. The one he has the most confidence in to head up the group that is responsible for designing the better system. This suggestion will usually be greeted with cries of anguish by the production control manager who will suggest that this man could head up the project part-time. This is not a practical approach, although tempting, since the day-to-day problems always have higher priority than the problem of designing systems. The man who is responsible for the systems design *must work on the project full-time and have no day-to-day responsibility!* Note that this man is the "indispensible" man in production and inventory control. Often not the manager of the department, but certainly his most likely successor. He too will need some education. He too will need to visit some other companies, learn about the software that the computer manufacturers have available, etc.

The company may at this point decide to engage a consultant. Most consultants will be only too happy to accept the task of designing the system for them since this means more resident consultants being "rented" out to the client. Actually, the client will be well advised to use the consultant only to advise and guide them. The client should insist on the highest caliber man available to work on the project. They should look into his credentials and check references with other companies he has worked with on the development of systems. They should *not* assume that since he works for a particular consulting company and "they stand behind him" that he is necessarily competent. He might have just come in off the street last week.[2]

Here the company faces a truly difficult dilemma. In this day of advanced technology and specialization, very few companies

---

[2] A man who was on his way to his first consulting assignment asked his supervisor if the client might not be dissatisfied with his background. He had spent all of his previous working years in one company and the consulting firm had given him no education before hustling him off on his first job. His supervisor's answer was "Don't worry, they won't even ask!"

can expect to have the technical knowledge required in all areas of management. Consulting firms should help to provide this. Unfortunately, sorting out the truly professional firms from the commercial firms is a most challenging task. Any business that is structured so that the executives in the business get additional monetary compensation based on the number of man days of consulting they can sell, invites abuses. The company should look for the consultant that is willing to act primarily as a catalyst. The consultant should help the people within the company to get what they want rather than trying to impose what he wants. Nevertheless, consultants should also try to steer the company away from reinventing the wheel and toward using fairly standard approaches to solve the problems of business which have not proven to be particularly unique from one company to another.

One last piece of advice repeated: Never assume that the consultant has responsibility for making the system work. Ultimately that will fall upon the company and the users of the system. There is no way that the manager can abdicate this responsibility or sub-contract it to an outsider in the final analysis.

A steering committee should now be considered. This could include responsible representatives of marketing, finance, engineering, and production as well as the production control manager. The man responsible for the systems design came from production control and he is now the chairman of the systems group and reports to the steering committee periodically.

Occasionally special sub-committees are set up. Assume, for example, that the new inventory system may require an entirely different approach to bills of material. At this point the engineering, marketing, and manufacturing group representatives, along with some special representatives from order entry, may form a special sub-committee to explore approaches to structuring bills of material and come back with their own recommendations. The main responsibility for the systems design, however, will reside with the representative of production and inventory control — where the real payoff results are expected to be generated.

Note the role of an ideal systems man in this project. He was the man aware of the potential of the computer who suggested that it would be used to get better results from the company. He probably contacts the consulting people and other companies that should be visited, suggests the kind of education available, and then acts as a catalyst himself, trying to get the reaction performed without performing it himself.

Hopefully, he recognizes that he is not an expert in any one of the areas where he is trying to generate more interest in improved approaches. He certainly is not an expert in quality control, nor is he an expert in production and inventory control; and the day he considers himself one, his ego has run away with him. He *is* aware of some of the things that can be done better in these areas. He is very cautious about accepting the things he has read and heard, since he suspects that most of the literature that comes across his desk is well laced with baloney. He also knows that when a system is completed, he will have contributed very substantially to its success by selling ideas and being the agitator for change and improvement. He probably will not get a great deal of credit because if the system is really successful, the users will claim it as their own and hardly recognize his contributions.

The systems man should also be a coordinator. He should try to avoid excessive amounts of duplication. If the new scrap reporting system can draw upon some information that could later be used for a production control shop floor control system, this is all well and good. He should not be a slave to "integrated systems." There will always be some duplication and some apparent inefficiencies. Stockholders can point out that the company is obviously wasting money because two separate letters were received in one day, each with a first class stamp affixed — and management has difficulty explaining that this may be the best and most economical way to run the company. The same is true of systems. There will always be some duplication. The important thing is not to run the data processing department most efficiently, but to get the information that is needed to run the company more efficiently.

The systems man has come in for a great deal of abuse in recent years. Management has often looked to him to improve their performance rather than asking themselves how they could use his talents to get these performance improvements themselves. There are no systems that will make business run better. There are only systems that will give people information to run businesses better. The responsibility for these systems rests with the management, not with the systems people. The good systems man trains himself to act as the catalyst. He swallows his ego frequently since he receives little credit for the successful system. But he and his associates in data processing are the people most likely to instigate change and improvement in most companies.

Note that not a great deal was said about the financial executive who had the computer and systems staff reporting to him. Many companies are very disturbed about the fact that their computer and systems staff report to financial people. They often contend that having the computer report to the financial executive results in getting the payroll, accounts receivable, and accounts payable on the computer rather than important applications. Actually, where the computer and systems staff reports is irrelevant. If the fact that they report to the financial executive results in having him use the computer for his own benefit rather than allocating systems effort where it will generate the most good for the company, he deserves to be demoted, given a green eyeshade and a quill pen. The same is true of any other executive who is given responsibility for the computer and then uses it only to satisfy his own needs rather than to satisfy the needs of the company. But most of the fault for this kind of perversion of the computer and the computer systems peoples' talents rests with general management because it has not taken positive action to get better performance and insisted on intelligent use of the computer to attain that better performance.

The group in the company used in the hypothetical example above will now proceed with their project. They may not be able to get the system implemented soon enough to give the production and inventory control manager the tools he needs to get better results this year. He may have to reassess the objectives set for him and postpone some of them. On the other hand, it is always well to remember that data processing and systems people tend to give extravagantly long estimates of the time required to do a job. Without adding an army of people, the revised inventory system should not take much more than six to twelve months. Later, systems for capacity planning and shop floor control could be added to this. They might take another six to twelve months to implement. These are obviously generalizations, and the implementation time can vary widely, depending on the availability of basic information (such as bills of material). But it may be well for the manager to have some benchmarks when he is given the too frequent estimate of "six to eight man years." Here again, it is well to remember that in most of the areas of manufacturing control, for example, the wheel has been invented and needs only minor tailoring to suit individual company requirements.

All through the development of the system it is well to keep the "indians" involved. These are the people who are out on the firing line and will actually have to use the results of the system. A great deal has been written about the need for education of systems users so that they fully understand what is being done. Education alone will not do the job; some *is* needed, but users who are thoroughly involved with the development of a system, understand its intent, and are not having an oversophisticated system foisted upon them, generally do not need a great deal of formal education in order to use systems intelligently.

Never disdain to consult with the indians. They often know a great deal more about what is going on in the real world than most people tend to recognize. After all, we must give them credit; they were able to run the company *in spite* of the previous systems.

And if the new system does not work out as well as we hope, we will probably have to depend upon them to bail us out again!

One last word of caution. That man we took out of the user group to put in charge of the system is in an area where the atmosphere is very heady. Very quickly other users will tend to disassociate him from the practical problems, and too often he will get caught up with the fascination of the computer and sophisticated systems. If the project is going to last for a long time, he should be moved back into the user group in about six months.[3] Very few people can fill the role of a "user" in a systems group for very long without becoming overly systems-oriented and disassociated from the users. In the case of a large company with a major project, rotating some of the people in and out of these two groups is the only hope for keeping user influence really predominant.

THE CORPORATE SYSTEMS GROUP

In any multi-division corporation it becomes apparent very quickly that divisional activities tend to overlap each other and a lot of duplication and wasted effort is going to result. Some companies, therefore, set up corporate systems groups. Like any activity this one can too easily become self-sustaining and lose its orientation with the real world. Large corporate systems groups and massive "total systems" or "management information systems" efforts generally have not proven to be profitable. As the pendulum has swung from having the divisions each go along their independent ways to having a corporation systems group trying to

---

[3] One of my friends, who is a real professional in the area of production and inventory control systems in a large corporation, has an interesting observation. He feels that any systems project that can't be broken down into modules taking less than six months each probably never will fly. There is some truth to this because of personnel turnover and the difficulty of maintaining contact and credibility with the users.

get all of the divisions to conform to an overall centrally conceived plan, it has become painfully obvious that there are a great many more wrong than right ways to approach this subject. It is too easy for a corporate systems group to start designing systems for the users rather than getting users involved in planning their own systems.

The proper role of the corporate systems group should be to

1. Generate ideas and foster communications among divisions.
2. Educate division people and refer them to competent outside sources for education.
3. Counsel divisions on which consulting firms are competent. Counsel also on how to use consulting.
4. Encourage standardization among divisions on
   (a) hardware,
   (b) programs,
   (c) terminology,
   (d) documentation of systems,
   (e) procedures, and
   (f) performance measures.
5. Encourage the development of long-range data processing systems plans.
6. Foster a business-like attitude toward computer systems. Operating management should be neither anti-computer nor starry-eyed. Systems/data processing people should be constantly educated and directed in order to keep them oriented toward the goals of the business.

The corporate systems manager is more likely to be successful if he is *not* a data processing/systems alumnus, but instead an ex-manager. This gains him credibility with other managers, and he is also more likely to have a real business outlook.

Obviously, he should have technical specialists on his staff. Some of them might even earn higher salaries than their manager (avoid promoting people whose real interest and competence are in their technical specialties to manage this group).

This group will probably include some specialists in areas like production and inventory control systems. These people must, of course, be good catalysts who are readily accepted as professionals by divisional people.

Some corporate staff consultants bill their time to divisions on a daily rate rather than just including their costs in an allocation of all corporate systems expenses to the divisions. This approach tends to keep corporate systems groups small and honest. It also tends to develop a man's selling talents!

One pitfall that the corporate systems group should avoid is premature centralization, even when there is obvious hardware duplication. It is hard enough to get successful operating systems going without adding the problem of remote data processing. The rule is simple: Learn how to make money with computers before concentrating on optimizing computer expense.

The corporate systems job is a tough one. Few have done it very successfully.[4] Above all, this group should be oriented toward business, not technical, objectives. Corporate systems groups should be small and composed of a few technical people directed by others who really understand the overall company goals and have an extraordinary talent for *selling* ideas to the managers who are responsible for company performance.

---

[4] The corporate systems group that was often discussed as a model of how to organize, etc., several years back belonged to Company A (see Chapter 1). This was the company that managed to parlay a 40 million dollar project into a 100 million dollar fiasco!

5

Designing Effective Systems

"A manager would rather live with a problem he cannot solve than accept a solution he cannot understand."

THE GRAND DESIGN

Before embarking on any systems project, we should try to plan how this project will fit into other systems efforts and what the long-range goals will be. It would be a good idea, for example, to know how the inventory system is going to fit into an overall production and inventory control system so that the inventory system will not have to be revised very dramatically when the production control systems of capacity planning and shop floor control are eventually established.

It would also be a good idea to plan how these systems are likely to fit into other efforts, such as the scrap reporting system,

97

and it would be well to consider how these systems will interface with payroll and accounting. Overlapping and duplication are inefficient. The amount of time and energy that is spent on the grand design, however, should be minimal. It will change as the needs of the business change and as knowledge about better potential applications is gained.

For many computer-oriented people the worst sin is to duplicate or overlap systems. They tend to put a great deal of stock in the importance of the grand design and the integrated system, in order to avoid this obvious inefficiency. To the operating man, the integrated system is a myth. He wants systems that work even if they do duplicate and even if the data processing equipment may not always be run at peak efficiency.

It is important to strike a balance between the two extremes. Duplication is undesirable. But, if we are going to have to wait to get all of the systems integrated into an ideally optimized system, the chances are the company will never see any tangible results. A little time spent on the grand design can be profitable. When the systems efforts become totally subordinated to an overall program and high payoff applications are postponed for the sale of integrating them more efficiently into an imagined future "total system," the company is being run for computer efficiency, not operating efficiency.

SYSTEMS SHOULD SUPPORT THE USER

When computers first started to be used in business, few companies knew what to do with them, what was practical, and what was not. A great deal of nonsense was written about the computer replacing the middle manager and automatically making decisions and controlling businesses. This has turned out to be a pipe dream. When people started to systematize some of the things that the middle manager or even the first-line supervisor did, they soon realized how little of his job was arithmetic and clearly defined logic, and found that most of it consisted of taking actions based on an understanding of the intent of the job and the situation at the moment. That situation was usually comprised of a great many variables, all interacting upon each other.

The uninitiated tend to think of business decisions as straightforward, clearly understood logic when, in fact, business decisions vary on a day-to-day basis because of varying situations.

Consider one apparently simple type of decision. Material requirements planning has been used as an example in this book. One of the features of this approach to inventory control is its ability to indicate when material needs to be rescheduled; either given an earlier or a later due date because requirements have changed. There has been a great deal of debate about whether or not it is feasible to let computers do the rescheduling. What are some of the things that could affect that decision in the real world?

The amount to be rescheduled. Certainly if the inventory position is one unit below the desired level and there is a safety stock, it would probably not be wise to reschedule the order for such a trivial requirement.

The remaining lead time for replenishing inventory. An inventory item that was not due for 30 weeks would probably not be rescheduled by any rational inventory planner, even if the system told the planner to change the schedule by plus or minus one week. When the lead time is that long, the chance that there will be other changes back and forth between now and the actual delivery date are great.

Relations with the vendor. It could be that this vendor has had to respond to a great deal of schedule changing recently and that any trivial reschedule might serve to aggravate vendor relations.

The load ahead of the vendor or the manufacturing department. If the department were looking for work, it might be well to reschedule a job. If they were already overloaded, improving the priority on one job might aggrevate an already bad situation.

The list of real-world considerations could be endless. This is not to say that people always do a good job of handling all of these considerations, but it certainly is not reasonable to expect that these considerations can be easily programmed into a computer once and for all. Most companies using a computerized material requirements planning program find that it is best to have the computer indicate that material needs to be rescheduled, and let people do the rescheduling. If the computer is to do any rescheduling, it should follow very simple rules so that the inventory planners still are "in control" — it doesn't take much sophistication to make the system unmanageable.

Frequently, systems people point to the fact that people do not do a very good job of executing the management policy, and they use this as a justification for trying to capture a great deal of day-to-day decision making within the computer. The facts are right but their conclusions are wrong. The fact that many people do not execute management policy properly usually indicates that management has not expressed this policy to them clearly. Take the example of the manager of a stockroom who is not at all concerned with keeping inventory records correctly, even though he controls the flow of documents in and out of the stockroom that actually update the inventory records. Why isn't he more conscious of his responsibility for the integrity of the inventory records? The answer is apparent. Management never explained it to him that way. He always found that he could blame someone else if the inventory records were off, and, in fact, in most cases he never did understand that it was his responsibility to handle the input documents properly to keep these inventory records accurate. No amount of systems work will correct basic problems of this type until management sets proper objectives. The systems man who tries to program his way around them is in for big disappointments.

One man who has done some writing recently said, "We will transfer the inventory decision responsibility to the computer."

That statement is patently ridiculous. Nobody is going to transfer inventory decision responsibility to a computer. The decision responsibility lies with people. The decision itself may be executed on the computer. The computer might do some analysis to help people make better decisions, but the responsibility for the decisions still must rest with people. Too often systems are designed with the idea that the computer will control; many inventory systems started this way. Computer systems designers assumed that the computer would actually do the ordering, but before installing this system they got "chicken." Very few companies actually let the computer place an order by itself. They usually have a human being review it. Too frequently, given the way the system has been designed the man cannot possibly make an intelligent review of the computer decision. Systems should be designed to help people control, rather than being designed around the naive idea that computers are actually going to control.

Systems must be designed for the user. The user has the responsibility — systems are merely tools to help him make better decisions. The user should be able to control any exceptions that he gets from the system, and he must be able to go into the computer to get further information when the information that he needs does not appear on the "exception reports" that fit some predetermined and usually simplistic logic. One item on an exception report can easily require further information on three or four more items that were not printed out on the exception logic.

This leads then to an important rule for computer systems design:

Make the Logic Obvious.

This rule, which might be called *the rule of system transparency,* underscores the need to have that user who has the responsibility for the system results understand the logic of the system. It is so easy to program logic into a computer. The computer is a compelling tool, and the man who understands the computer is often fascinated by the intellectual challenge of using its capabilities in a more sophisticated manner. However, without any real effort on the systems man's part, he can sophisticate his system to the point that the logic is no longer obvious. This leaves the user with the classical dilemma of either ignoring the system completely or following it blindly.

The vice president of a large pharmaceutical house stated recently that automation had been a disappointment to them. They found, for example, that they could mix batches of their compounds automatically and control quality with more precision than they could manually. But they also found that when they started mixing batches automatically, the machine operator assumed no responsibility for the activity. If something went wrong in the control system and the liquid filled the vat beyond its normal capacity, the operator tended not to notice this until the vat overflowed onto the floor. The vice president indicated that his company is very distressed about his people's lacking a sense of responsibility for "automatic" systems. As a result, they are putting more of the operation of the system back into the hands of the user. We certainly have had the same problem with computerized information systems. And this leads to a second rule concerning user orientation of the system:

Do not remove control and assume that the user will still accept responsibility.

Until the time when systems can control businesses 100 percent (if that *ever* happens) the main role of computerized systems should be to provide better information to help people in doing their jobs. The whole system should be designed around people and not around computers. The computer can massage arithmetic and reference files far more effectively than the human being can. The human being can deal with an unstructured, ever-changing real world far better than the computer can. The best systems are those that most successfully combine these capabilities of the machine and the man.

Many managers have embraced computer systems as an escape from the frustration of directing people to do tasks. They have learned that they do not escape the people problems and, in fact, encounter a whole new set of machine-oriented people problems in addition to the ones they already had.

DESIGNING SYSTEMS FOR CONTROL

As the computer developed, "systems" soon became a major area of activity in business. But too much time has been spent *doing* — usually unsuccessfully — and very little in the way of system design principles has been developed. Unfortunately, there has been too much systems work and too little thinking about the basic structure of control systems.

Any control system should be built around four basic elements. These are

1. A norm.
2. Tolerance.
3. Feedback.
4. Action.

The wall thermostat is a good example of a simple control system. A norm is set. This is the temperature we would like to maintain in the room. The tolerance is set because it would be impractical to have a furnace going on and off with every fraction of a degree change in temperature. Therefore, this type of control system is usually designed so that the temperature can vary about two degrees before the furnace will respond. Feedback exists in the form of a thermometer. It measures the temperature and compares it against the norm minus its tolerance. Action takes place whenever the system detects that the temperature is below the norm minus the tolerance.

That all seems elementary, doesn't it? Yet consider the types of information we see around us. One report that many manufacturing companies use, for example, is a "purchase commitment report." This shows the material that is on order, the vendors who are to supply it, and the amount of dollars that are "committed" in each future month. An interesting piece of information for the financial officer, who can use this to help in determining how much cash outgo the company is going to have in future months.

This is also an interesting example of the typical accounting type of information built around "scorekeeping" rather than control. That is not to say that some scorekeeping is not needed, but the real question is whether or not the amount of material on order is the right amount of material. Where is the *norm* in this? Who has said how much material *should* be on order? And outside of providing interesting information to the financial officer, what action does this information indicate? Here is a good example of the undirected, ill-thought-out approach to information management. Jules Henri Poincaré, the French mathematician, said, "Science is built of facts as a house is built of bricks, but a heap of facts is no more a science than a heap of bricks a house."

A heap of information is no more a control system than a dictionary is a shelf of novels, even though it contains all the words required to make the novels. The purchase commitment report could be a much more valuable report if it were broken down by product groups, so that we could evaluate information based on the current sales of manufacturing rate, how many dollars should be coming into inventory, and set that as a norm. The feedback on the actual purchase commitments could then be compared against that. A pre-determined tolerance could be set to determine when the system is considered sufficiently out of control to justify taking action and that action should be *pre-planned*. If, for example, the purchase commitment report shows that a particular product line has more dollars coming in than was planned, the inventory manager might instruct his planner to review certain items to see if they could be rescheduled for a later date.

Think of the typical machine load report. It shows the number of hours due to be produced in each week. It hardly represents a realistic plan, since these hours are likely to vary significantly from week to week. Everyone who has ever worked in a factory knows how difficult and expensive it is to change production rates. A realistic plan would show a fairly level production rate over a long period of time — a realistic *norm*. And the typical machine load report in most manufacturing companies does not show the actual production for any period of time; very few of them are likely to show the actual output for more than one week. This is not a long enough length of time to determine the rate of output, since in any individual week there could be excessive machine breakdowns, excessive absentism, or an unusually fortunate circumstance of high productivity. Three to four weeks of output history is needed to determine what the real production rate of a facility, such as a work center, truly is.

Lacking a realistic norm and indicative feedback, it's hardly worth talking about the lack of tolerance in the machine load report. The fact of the matter is that the machine load reports in most companies simply do not generate action and that they were never designed as *control* systems.

It is worth addressing this problem of *tolerance* briefly. Think, for example, of a capacity plan that indicates the number of hours a work center should be producing each week. At what point should action be taken, if the work center is underproducing or overproducing? Certainly a work center that is supposed to turn out 150 hours per week will not be asked to take corrective action if total production for the last three weeks has been 448 hours! On the other hand, if production had only been 200 hours for the last three weeks, a serious situation could exist. What should the tolerance be? Here is where the mathematicians could have a field day. But the important point is not to have a scientifically accurate tolerance, but to have one that is rational and close enough for all practical purposes. Tolerances do not need to be precise but they should be agreed on ahead of time. Too frequently the weekly production meeting in a manufacturing company turns out to be a donneybrook because people have not agreed ahead of time on the tolerance they will allow in the system (and they usually do not have a very good control system to begin with). A realistic planned production rate should be set and the actual production rate compared with it. A realistic tolerance should then be agreed upon ahead of time. This is not the type of thing to be decided at *the weekly* production meeting.

It is important to set tolerances realistically. Very often, for example, the engineer sets idealistic manufacturing tolerances that cannot possibly be attained with the equipment in the factory. The foreman, recognizing that these are unrealistic tolerances, tries to do the best job he can, and when the job is inspected, rather than scrap it, a deviation from specification is obtained in order to pass the job. What a lot of nonsense to go through because realistic tolerances were not set in the first place! But this type of situation is common in almost every human endeavor. When the engineer finds that the job was not made to the idealistic tolerances that he set, more than likely he will come up with a clever reaction that he thinks is fairly original and creative. He will set the tolerances tighter the next time. The foreman, of course, by this time has no regard for tolerances at all and knows that engineering is either naive or doesn't really mean what they say.

This type of situation can be seen repeatedly from company to company. How many companies, for example, generate a massive expedite report and give it to the purchasing department. There isn't a prayer that the purchasing department could expedite all the jobs on the list so they ignore the report completely and call the manufacturing people to find out which parts they really need. There is a kind of Gresham's law that exists with systems — *the realistic tolerances will supplant the unrealistic tolerances in the day-to-day operation of the system.* Tolerances need to be set realistically and to be enforced. When the formal system tolerances are unrealistic, there are *no* tolerances. When management does not take action, when tolerances are exceeded, they have publicly announced that they do not believe in the tolerances. From that point on the system will no longer do much to help management control.

No system will really generate control information effectively if it does not have a norm, feedback, tolerances, and a pre-planned action that is to be taken when the system shows that the situation is out of control. The time for a firedrill is before the fire starts so that, when there really is a problem, people will know how to react. A great many companies spend more time debating whether or not they have problems than they do solving the problems. The result is to let little problems fester and develop into major crises before they actually do anything.

In addition, systems response should be tuned to the environment. Consider an inventory system that can recalculate priorities every week. Assume that there is a dispatch list that goes to the factory floor daily. As long as there is more than one job sitting ahead of an operation, the changes in priorities on the daily dispatch list can tell the shop people which jobs really should be started next. The shop then has an automated system that can respond to rapid changes in priority. Purchasing, on the other hand, may have to handle all the reschedules manually by calling vendors on the telephone. It is important to be careful not to give purchasing a great deal of trivial reschedules until they have a better capacity for reacting.

Many systems have generated more confusion than results because the inexperienced systems designer got carried away with the computer's ability to generate control information and ignored the ability of the people to react to this volume of information. Once again, realistic tolerances are needed to avoid an overly "nervous" system.

SYSTEMS SHOULD BE MODULAR

Initial experiences with the attempts at totally "integrated" information systems were very sad indeed. Those that were somewhat integrated turned out to be impossible to modify without tearing the whole system apart and putting it back together again. Assume that there is an inventory system with an item master record. This item master record contains basic inventory information as well as accounting information that can be used for product cost buildup such as labor, material, and overhead. If it is decided to use this record for accounting information, the programs that draw information from the same basic master record should be *independent*. If they are designed and maintained as independent programs, it will be possible to change the accounting program without changing the inventory program and vice versa.

By the same token the inventory program should be modular itself. Such things as order quantity calculations should not be built into the program ahead of time. Instead the item master record can have codes in it that can be varied item by item to use a number of different order quantity sub-routines. There should be an exit from the main-line program so that an unlimited number of sub-routines can be used and can be modified without having to restructure the entire inventory control program. Some of these sub-routines may not be written when the original program is written and they may not be written for a number of years in the future. The system that is designed properly will have this modular capability.

One company was giving serious consideration to an automatic specification program. In this program a customer's product requirements would be fed into the computer. The computer, using some product specification logic and reference tables, would specify the bill of materials for the configuration of the product to be supplied. It was proposed that this automatic specification program would then go directly into a master schedule that would then go directly into the requirements planning type inventory system. One big program? Potentially one big mess! Actually, the program should be developed in modules. The specification system should be separate from the master schedule system, which should be a separate entity by itself and separate from the inventory control system. Obviously these programs must interface, but they should not be included in one big program.

Why the emphasis on modularity? Because *change is the only constant* in real-world systems. Even if the perfect system were someday developed, people would want to make it better. This is the very nature of people and, as a consequence, the very nature of business. Systems must be modular to facilitate change and ease of installation.

Perhaps even more important is the need to have *milestones* in systems development and implementation. Many companies have embarked on ambitious, well-intentioned systems development efforts that went completely out of control. Management with all good intentions allocated the money in an attempt to make the business better, yet after long periods of investing money without seeing a return they had no way to know whether or not any progress was being made. Systems should be developed and implemented on a modular basis with *milestones* along the way so that management can know whether or not progress is actually being made. The "taste of success" can contribute powerfully to user support of systems. Any system that cannot be broken down into reasonable modules is probably just a designer's pipe dream.

INUNDATED WITH PAPER

If there is any threat to the world's forests more serious than any natural pestilence in history, it is the high-speed computer printer and systems designed without a healthy concern for the amount of paper being put out. Early punched card and computer applications tended to require a great deal of paper output. Consider the example of an inventory application.

A manually posted inventory record had advantages as well as disadvantages. While no great amount of computation could be done and it was subject to clerical error, it did have the advantage of "random access"; the planner could go to the record anytime and read it. It also provided an audit trial. He could not only look at the inventory balance today, but he could determine *how* each inventory transaction had changed the record to get it to where it is today.

Along came the computer. There were obvious advantages to putting this record into it. Things like requirements planning that were not even feasible, manually, could be done. In addition, there were fewer clerical errors. But how about the frequency of output? If the manual record is now replaced by a computer inventory record, how often will inventory balances be printed out? When will they be available to the user? How will he get an effective audit trail to check the integrity of his records?

Frequently, systems are designed so that there is a weekly printout. Depending on the number of inventory records and the amount of paper one item takes, there could be a vast amount of printout. It is not unusual in a requirements plan, for example, to have the amount of detail on each item planned requiring one full page of printout. A company with 20,000 to 30,000 items could have a mountain of paper easily five feet high coming out of the computer each week.

There are other problems too. Now the user wants to know in the middle of the week what the inventory balance is. He has no way of getting it, and it is not practical to print out a complete requirements plan for each item each day! It might be feasible to print out inventory balances each day because this would require far less paper, but even that would be rather tedious and awkward to work with.

And what of that audit trail? That could be printed out on a daily basis for the previous day's transactions. But if an audit trail were printed out for each item that had activity each day, by the end of the week the inventory planner would have to look through five separate reports to check on one item. And what of the previous week's history? Where would that be? Obviously, this could all be sorted down by item and summarized into one report so that he could reference it more easily, but now, once again, we have generated mountains of paper.

Early in the computer game, the idea of exception reports came along. But, in point of fact, there is a lot more talk about exception reports than actual implementation and for good reason. It is well to theorize about the reasons for creating an exception report but, in fact, it is very difficult to come up with rules that apply all the time. Consider, for example, an inventory report that prints out only those items that require action, such as ordering or rescheduling. The planner looks at an item and in checking it out with the factory he finds that it is not only running behind schedule, it has in fact been scrapped. This part goes into a sub-assembly. The sub-assembly did not print out on this run because there was no reason to have a printout. At this point the planner needs some way to look at the sub-assembly inventory record, even though the exception reporting rules did not make it available to him. The problem is a simple one: It is not too difficult to define the general rules to follow in determining what information should be generated so that people will take action; it is *very difficult*, however, to determine what information they are likely to need for legitimate reference purposes.

Even when exception reporting is used it can get to be burdensome. Assume that there is an item that should be rescheduled according to some simple rules. The inventory planner has some additional information and has decided not to reschedule. How can the system be told not to print this out and keep telling the planner each week that the item needs to be rescheduled? The obvious answer is a flag in the inventory file to indicate that it does not need to be printed out as an action report until another transaction of any type affects the record. "Exception reports by the ream" are more often the rule than the exception.

These are very definitely problems. Fortunately, today there are solutions to these problems. This is not the place to explore all the innovations in technology, since this book does not address computer hardware or software, but two examples of modern technology are worth discussing briefly. The visual display unit or CRT (Cathode Ray Tube) has become a fairly common device. It can be used to inquire into records that are maintained on disc files. Many systems use these CRT's today and they represent a real step forward since the user once again has random access as he did with his manual records. They have become a practical device that is relatively inexpensive in most applications and almost invariably popular with the user.

Another step forward in technology is microfilm. Microfilm, of course, has been around for years and most people view it as a way to condense archives. It can be used for a lot more than that today. Rather than printing a report on paper a company can generate it on magnetic tape. Practically every large city now has a service bureau that will pick up this magnetic tape, convert it to microfilm and have it back, usually, overnight. Relatively inexpensive microfilm viewers that look almost exactly like CRT's can be used to view the microfilm conveniently. Viewers are obtainable which can reproduce the image on the screen on a piece of paper if necessary. Microfilm is relatively inexpensive. Often the savings in forms paper will practically defray the cost of the microfilm system. For computers that are not operating in a multi-programming mode the savings in print time can be substantial also, since it takes far less time for a computer to transfer data onto magnetic tape than it does to print.

Using microfilm, for example, a weekly requirements plan could be printed out with the *exceptions only* printing. The balance of the requirements plans could be generated on microfilm so that they would be available for reference. The inventory records could be generated on microfilm once or twice during the week, if this were necessary.

For those companies that have large enough computers to use CRT's, a combination of CRT's and microfilm can work out very well. A typical application might be as follows:

1. The requirements plan is done by exception each night, only for those items that have activity. Paper is generated only for these items.

2. CRT's are available to inquire into the inventory files at anytime. These are available to the planners, and at least one of them in the inventory control office has a copier on it.

3. Transaction histories for the current week are kept on the inventory files. They can be inquired into via the CRT's. Transaction histories for the last two months are kept on microfilm. Each week a new tape is created and a new microfilm is made up.

There are many possibilities today for designing systems that generate a minimum of paper work. This not only saves money, it just plain makes sense. Nothing is so discouraging to see as mountains of paper. Nothing looks quite so disorganized or confused as an office with stacks and stacks of dog-eared data processing reports sitting around. Down with paper!

DESIGNING INTEGRITY INTO THE SYSTEM

One of the toughest things to show managers is the relationship between basic system integrity and results. Many managers, for example, during a cost cutting period will reduce the number of people being used to maintain basic information such as bills of material. Later on they will wonder why they cannot get the right parts needed to get the product out the door on time and why so many people are spending time fire fighting because the system does not function properly.

Probably one of the most difficult areas to get management interested in is stockrooms. The component parts stockroom in most manufacturing companies is a disgrace. Somehow it seems easier to program complex mathematical inventory computations into a system than to put a fence around the stockroom and teach the stockroom people to control the flow of paper with the flow of materials so that inventory records can be maintained correctly! There is little real value in inventory computations that start with inventory balance figures that are not accurate.

Many people in management find it difficult to see the relationship between accurate inventory records and performance. In a company that makes an assembled product, for example, lack of one component can result in the worst of all possible worlds; inventory will be high, due to the presence of all other components, service will be low because the product cannot be shipped. One of the most profitable places for attention is stockrooms, yet it seems to be too unromantic an area for most people even to think about. Most systems people would rather sit down and draw flow charts than get down to the nasty business of showing management where attention is really needed if systems are going to work properly.

The first thing required if a system is going to have integrity is concern for this integrity on the part of the systems designers and management. Time and again systems efforts are put into the computer programs — which undoubtedly will work right eventually — while very little effort is put into the difficult areas that involve people, like the stockroom, that more often than not are the real causes for systems downfall! Chapter 7 will deal at length with the problem of *maintaining* systems integrity because it relates to the problem of learning to manage a business with a system. Some techniques can be used to *design* integrity into the system.

Audit trails were mentioned above. This is a very practical

way to assist the user in validating the records. Tests of reasonableness can be built into a system. The stock clerk posting a manual inventory record could often detect that a transaction was ridiculous just because the quantity was unreasonably high. The computer can detect this also if someone can define "unreasonable" in terms of numbers.

Here again no great amount of knowledge about the computer is required to know that it can compare a receipt with any other number or any product of other numbers that are already in the inventory file. If there is an inventory record that shows the average withdrawals per month, some number limits can be established such as "3 times the monthly average," and the computer can check each receipt to see that it does not exceed this number. If the computer record shows accumulated receipts to date, the program can be written so that the computer converts this into an average and uses it to compare the receipts against it. On the other hand if this is a requirements planning type inventory system the computer could compare an individual receipt with the next three (or four or five, etc.) months' gross requirements. The only problem is to think through the logic and give the computer some rules to work with so that it can create exception notices. Then it becomes important for the planner to have some type of audit trail so that he can verify the transaction.

One of the standard techniques for culling out common transposition errors is the *check digit.* Assume that the part number is 138209. A check digit can be calculated for this part number as follows:

Step 1. Starting with the right-hand digit, and proceeding from *right to left,* double every other digit. If there is a quantity to be carried, it should be carried to the next digit to be doubled.

Part number 1 3̲ 8 2̲ 0 9̲
                 6   5   8

Step 2. Insert the digits that have not been doubled, 168508.

Step 3. Add these digits up. The total equals 28.

Step 4. Subtract the last digit of the result from 10 to obtain a check digit:

$$10 - 8 = 2.$$

Two is now the check digit. Look at any credit cards you have. They usually use this kind of check digit. When a charge is being entered against someone's account, the keypunch operator punches the credit card number. The keypunch itself has an attachment which goes through the little algorithm above and calculates the check digit. When the operator gets to the check digit itself, if the digit that she punches into the card does not equal the digit that the machine calculates, it will signal an error.

One company uses check digits in their stockrooms. A good many stockroom errors occur when the wrong item is pulled from its location. This can cause two errors because the part actually withdrawn does not have its inventory record relieved while the part number that was transmitted in error does relieve an inventory record that should not have been relieved. This company has calculated a check digit for each of their part numbers. That digit appears on the bin where the part is located. When the stockman pulls material from a bin he must note the digit on the requisition (the digit does not appear on the master parts list that he would normally use to fill out a requisition for an unplanned transaction). When the part number is key punched the check digit is calculated. If the digit that was on the bin does not coincide, obviously the stock picker did not pick the right part or the number was incorrect on the requisition. This is immediately followed up to determine exactly what the error was and get the record corrected.

Hash totals are another technique for maintaining system integrity. Whenever data such as source documents (receipts into the stockroom, for example) are being transferred from one location to another (from the stockroom to key punching) a *hash total* is generated. This is a piece of data — such as the quantity received — totalled by the group sending the documents. This is a meaningless ("hash") total, but if the receivers will run an adding machine tape from the documents they receive and compare the hash totals they can readily determine whether or not all the documents sent were actually received.

There are many techniques for designing integrity into a system. A few examples have been presented above simply to emphasize the importance of this consideration.

One last caution. Some systems designers try to develop elaborate systems solutions to basic operating problems. Consider the stockroom problem mentioned several times in this book. No amount of clever systems design will completely solve the problem of inventory record integrity if there is not the physical means to ensure that the paper moves as the material moves in and out of the stockroom. Stockroom fences do not generate accuracy by themselves; they do provide the stockroom manager the means for assuming the responsibility for transaction integrity. Systems design is not the way to solve this kind of problem; these basic operating problems must be solved *before* a system can be effective.

LET'S DO IT!

It's important to get a group out of planning mode and into action mode. This is sometimes difficult to do. Too many people on the committee or "team" can make a very confusing situation, particularly if each of them wants to design his own system. Nothing can delay a project like having too many systems people involved.

Another sure fire way to slow things down is to fail to clearly define responsibility. This needs to be pinned down as precisely as possible, always keeping in mind Boss Kettering's famous comment (when told that Lindberg had flown the Atlantic solo): "I'd have been more surprised if a committee had done it!"

At this point it is good to ask three questions whenever different phases of design come up. They are

1. What?
2. How?
3. Who?

What are we trying to do in this phase of the systems design? How are we going to go about it? Who is going to handle this part of the problem? So often people get bogged down discussing *who* and *how* before they have even determined *what*. Next time there is a fruitless confused discussion, try these three questions out and see if they do not help to show a path out of the confusion.

At this point somebody will probably come up with the bright idea that the present system should be completely analyzed and documented. This can take six months to six years and is usually a complete waste of time, particularly since the present system is about to be replaced. It was probably a formal system that never worked anyway. Whatever you do, do not get involved in a big boondoggle where people paste forms on a board with arrows showing which copy goes where. Many companies have done this. In order to save time it would be better to borrow one of these exhibits from another company and show it to the people who suggested documenting how the present system works. Without any question, the big "superflow chart" was never looked at too closely in the other company and nobody in your company is going to look too closely at it either.

In fact, if you want to do something really productive concerning the present system, you ought to find out how it *really* works. Go talk to the foreman, talk to the stockpickers, talk to the salesmen out in the field, see how these people on the firing line actually use the information that they get. Nine times out of ten you will find that they have their own ways of getting around the formal system and have developed informal, yet practical systems — at least from their viewpoint. These systems usually do not do the complete job, but they do enable the man on the firing line to survive, in spite of formal systems that often do even less of the job. The objective in developing a new system should be to close the gap between the formal and informal system.

Many people start by trying to design the files, under the mistaken concept that because the files have to be set up first they need to be designed first. No architect starts by designing the foundation of a building, even though the foundation must be put in before the building is put up. The output reports should be designed first. Then, the files that support these output reports should be designed. A few well-intentioned systems people, who believe all the MIS baloney they have been reading, feel that establishing a "data base" of files will enable them to get "any reports they require," so they put their time into establishing these files rather than into determining the actual information needs of the managers. This is a great way to waste a great deal of time. While files must be installed first, they should not usually be designed first. The first problem is to determine what the output must be — *then* the files can be developed.

When a formal system is replacing an informal system files need to be more accurate than they were in the past. This takes time and effort — if it is not included in the system design plan the systems will limp at best.

One last caution. In the enthusiasm of designing a system, ask at least once a day if the users are *really* involved, if they are *really* committed, if they *really* understand. It is easy to diagnose this as one of the causes for failure after a system has been installed. It is a lot more difficult to observe that this problem is occuring while the system is being developed.

Some kind of project plan would be worthwhile at this point. There are many project planning techniques available and they can be referenced in many other texts. The simplist is a Gantt chart — a simple bar chart showing both how long a particular element of the project is planned to take and how long it actually has taken. There are more sophisticated approaches to project planning (such as critical path analysis) but there are really very few practical computer application projects for the average company that warrant this kind of sophisticated planning.

It is a good idea, then, for the steering committee to have meetings regularly that review progress. The man in charge of the programs should make up a regular report, brief in nature, showing these elements in the chart that are not proceeding according to plan. He should also indicate why they are not proceeding according to plan and what needs to be done to get back on the plan. Actually, this is an ideal kind of job for a production control man whose main job is planning, monitoring, and pointing out the problems that occur in the day-to-day business of manufacturing.

The important contribution of the executive at this point is impatience. A desire to get the group moving and start generating results. Just as an engineering group can take forever to introduce a new product if they are not prodded, a systems design team can easily avoid getting into action mode. There are a million excuses, including the paralyzing fear of making a mistake. The major mistakes have been covered in earlier chapters; the minor ones are not worth worrying about. *Let's do it!*

6

Implementing the System

Best is the enemy of better.

GETTING INTO IMPLEMENTATION MODE

There comes a point in time when the design phase has to stop and implementation has to begin. Sometimes drawing this line is very difficult. It is very tempting to try to solve *all* the problems of the company. And, in fact, many of the users tend to encourage this approach with systems people. They are looking for systems that will relieve them of their problems, rather than tools to make the handling of their problems a little more systematic and fruitful. There are no perfect systems. If we wait for this kind of system, we will wait forever.

One of the most competent automotive engineers of the

1920's, Harold Wills, provides a lesson for everyone who will ever participate in the design of anything. In spite of his competence, in spite of his ability to manage and direct people, in spite of his financial backing and his genius in the design of automobiles, he was never able to produce a car of his own on a profitable basis. In fact, the company that he ran briefly, after working for Ford for many years, never produced very many cars at all. And one of the major reasons was simply that he never got out of the "design mode." He was continually designing the car even as it was going down the production line, always looking for the perfect car and never quite practical enough to freeze the design, imperfect as it was, and get it into production.

People who are designing systems should not wait to solve all the problems. The objective is not to achieve a utopia, it is just to make things better than they were yesterday.

PROGRAMMERS CAN PRODUCE

The typical company that cannot seem to get anything done in the data processing department automatically assumes that they need more programmers. Actually, programmers are probably the most under-utilized resource that exists in industry today. Here is a three-step program for getting programs written quickly and successfully.

1. *Make the user available to the programmer.* The user who knows what he wants and is responsible for, the system should sit with the programmer (or programmers) while they work on the system. Do not try to cover all of the details of the system design in the specifications. You simply cannot anticipate all the questions that will come up. How about the systems man? Should he be in on these discussions? Certainly he should be. He is the go-between, the catalytic agent between the user and the programmer. (It is quite possible that it may be a good idea to get him

out of the picture after he has gotten the ball rolling. Once the user and the programmer really understand how to communicate with each other, the systems man can often move on to other projects while occasionally checking to see how this system is progressing.)

Obviously this approach works best in a small or medium-sized company or where the system has been broken down into manageable modules. In large companies, with large systems projects, the principle is still valid although more difficult to implement.

One approach that does not usually work very well is to insist that the user write a highly detailed, completely comprehensive specification and give it to a programming group he has little contact with. Unless all problems, trade-offs, and misunderstandings can be foreseen, this approach, besides taking a very long time, tries to circumvent the very type of teamwork that is really the key to getting good results quickly.

Making the user available to the programmer whenever he wants him can make the programming progress very quickly indeed. When the programmer can refer to the user and get his questions answered quickly he can save both a lot of time spent pondering and a lot of false starts.

2. *Give the programmers plenty of test time.* Time and again, you can see programming managers hiring more programmers when they have not yet figured out how to give the programmers they have sufficient test time to make them productive. Programming is like any other activity that requires deep concentration. The start-up time can be very long indeed. Getting his mind trained on the problem, figuring out where he was when he stopped, and starting out all over again are extremely time-consuming activities for the programmer. If he works on his program and then must stop for two days while he waits for test time on the computer, he will have lost his train of thought. And once he does test, he will waste a great deal of time figuring out where he was and getting started all

over again. Test time should be available at a very minimum of once a day, preferably even twice a day, and any urgent project should be given very high priority.

Providing test time is easier said than done, of course, but now is a good time to try the favorite gambit of the systems man looking for time on the computer; try not sending out some of those reports that you suspect that nobody is really using anyway.

3. *Give the programmer an environment where he can concentrate.* The programming office in most companies is a most distracting environment. Certainly not the environment to encourage real concentration. There is almost always somebody with an interesting gossip tidbit to pass along that he just picked up over the phone or read in the latest magazine. There is almost always somebody coming in to ask for something or to ask how something is going. For some projects, where you really want to get some programming done quickly, it is often practical to pull the programmers you need out of the bull pen and put them in a conference room with the user until they get the job done.

With this approach major programs that often take a year in some companies can be accomplished in three or four months. Be very careful, however, when asking programmers to make time estimates. Somebody long ago told all the programmers in the world that if they ever missed a deadline they would be lined up against a brick wall and shot. Since that day, hardly a man among them has ever dared to make a realistic estimate for fear he would possibly miss the deadline. Most programming estimates start with a six-month miminum, for anything more complex than adding an asterisk, and go on from there to two or three years. Check around with others who have put in similar types of programs if you feel that you are not getting a realistic estimate of the programming time required for your system.

HOW ARE WE DOING?

One of the most neglected tools of management is performance measures. Just about everybody knows that when people are measured they will normally perform better. If you go into the typical company, it is not at all unusual to find very few performance measures, and very few of these are truly meaningful to the people who have to perform.

Before putting in a system, it is important to make sure that there are performance measures on vital functions. In the case of a material requirements planning type inventory control system for example, the kinds of improvements that should result are

1. Improved customer service.
2. Reduced inventory.
3. Increased assembly productivity.
4. Possible reductions of material handling by stockroom and inventory control personnel.

It is important to have some present measurements of performance, if any improvements are to be discerned. There should be a base reference period against which the system can be compared. This base reference period is pretty easy to establish. One of the biggest problems, however, with putting this system in is actually gauging performance measures. Systems do not get installed in laboratory type environments. The product line may increase dramatically, the method of distribution change, and a new plant may be built or several new warehouses added. It is important to establish the conditions that existed during the base reference period and to predict the impact that more new products or other foreseeable changes could have on the performance measures. This will not be precise, but some prediction of possible consequences will add credulity if it becomes necessary to explain why system performance has not been up to expectations and the real reason is a change in environment.

This is not the place to talk about performance measures in any great detail, but one thing should be pointed out. No performance measure is really all encompassing. Consider the apparently simple problem of measuring customer service. One of the most common measures in service is "line items shipped." This simply means that if a customer order comes in with ten items on it and nine of them were in stock, the company was able to give 90 percent service. This service measure does not take into account the duration of the stockout. If the item that was not shipped has been out of stock for some time, it may cause considerable customer annoyance, a great deal more annoyance than an item that has been out of stock for only a short period of time. If the item that has been out of stock for a long period of time is an extremely popular one — one of the "bread and butter" items in the product line — it could cause even more annoyance. If the customer is one of the company's biggest customers, this stockout could be even more important. Unfortunately, there is no way to take all of these items into consideration. Simple measures that provide a reasonable indication of the relative levels of performance are the best. Companies that have tried to develop complex composite index numbers to measure many facets of their customer service performance usually wind up with meaningless nonsense.

The point then is to measure present performance and predict what the system will enable people to do to improve performance. Objectives should be set and assigned to individuals who will then be responsible for attaining them. They should agree that these are reasonable objectives, in fact, a responsible, ambitious management setting these objectives should have been the prime mover behind the systems effort in the first place.

PROCEDURES — WHO READS THEM!

It is pathetic to consider the hours and hours of man effort that have been put into writing user operating procedures in company after company, when those procedures usually just get stuck in a drawer someplace, seldom get updated, and practically never referred to. One of the reasons for this, of course, is the grand old American tradition of never reading the instructions until all other approaches have failed.

User operating procedures then should be brief; they should be terse. Any procedure that takes over half an hour to read is probably too complicated anyway. These procedures should not be written by technical people unless they are very practically oriented. They should be written by operating people; the man who writes procedures should have a keen ability to separate the vital from the trivial. He should be sure that each procedure spells out its intent, its objectives, before going into great detail. Once again, a good sequence to follow is: What, How, Who?

There is a trend today toward having "mini-procedures" included right in program output. For example, an inventory stock-status report would have on its last page a definition of each of the fields and an explanation of how the information is put together, where it comes from, etc. This is a nuisance to keep up to date, but it is a lot more likely to be read than any detailed procedures.

While it is important then to have procedures, they should be brief, to the point, and they should spell out the system's intent. The manager of the department should run periodic education sessions when there are different people in the department, review various sections of the procedures, and explain how they are being handled in order to refresh people's memories. In other words, do not wait for people to come to the procedures, make the procedures go to them.

EDUCATION IS A NECESSITY — NOT A LUXURY

A great many thinking people today acknowledge that the colleges and universities have made a botch of business education. Business itself has nothing to brag about. Whom do we usually have handling education in a company, if indeed it is being handled at all? This is usually a job for the ex-college professor who has come to industry to get some of that "big money" that he keeps hearing about, or it is a place to put old Charlie who is not quite ready for retirement and needs something to keep him busy for the next eighteen months. One of the most successful companies in the country takes a far different approach. The most successful foreman in that company is given the job of educating other foremen for one to two years before he is moved on to the job of general foreman. The complete reversal of the old Anglo-Saxon tradition that: "He who can, does. He who cannot, teaches." Really, teaching should be entrusted to those who can *do* better than anyone else.

But what about education for the system? This may be fit into a continuing education program within the company, and, if there is a really successful program of this type, some professional help from the educators may be worthwhile. But the people who should do the educating are the users, not the systems people. Here again the systems people should "teach the teachers" and organize the education — acting as catalysts. For example, if a shop floor control system is being developed, make sure that the foremen who have been on the systems design team and who have had the responsibility for the system (since they are the real *users)* are the men who tell the other foremen about the system. Education should be brief and interesting. If there are two foremen to choose from to do the education, try to pick the one who is the best communicator. Give him a hand with his talk, however, since he probably has not done this type of thing very often. He probably will have a great deal of difficulty separating the vital from the trivial. One of the best ways to get an education program really going is to encourage a very short presentation followed by plenty of questions. Two-way communication is far better education than just listening.

Be sure to segregate people for education purposes. *Don't, for example, have a group of foremen sitting in with the general foreman and the plant superintendent and the plant manager and the general manager.* This kind of education program will be practically useless since there will be little or no discussion and participation. The foremen are not too likely to ask questions or participate very vigorously since they do not want to look foolish in front of all of that "brass." It probably never occurs to them that the reason the brass are being so quiet is they are afraid to look foolish in front of the people who work for them! One certain way to make an education program fail is to get programmers and systems people mixed in with people like foremen. Their interests are completely different and, if you satisfy either one of them, you will bore the other group to death.

Do not forget to include all of the people you should in the education program. Usually a computer system crosses many departmental lines and depends on many people to make it successful. Explain to the engineers and the salesmen, the order entry people, the shop foremen, and the accounting people what the new inventory system will be doing, how it will be dependent on them, and solicit their participation at the earliest stages of system design. Make sure that the "indians" — those people on the firing line who really keep a company running — understand what is going on. Systems activity always looks menacing to them. They see ominous signs in the comings and goings of corporate systems people, consultants, and others that they often tend to loosely lump into the category of "efficiency experts." Let them know quickly what your intentions are so that they do not have to speculate. Make it clear to them that you are not out to reduce the payroll (assuming that you are not and you probably are not very likely to with most computer systems).

Here again, the key to real education is participation. This is a place where a consultant also might be of some value to you. He could come in and help with some of the basic education although he should not be entrusted with the job of telling people about *your* system. This should be left to your people. The consultant should be able to make some points more effectively than people inside the company, partly because he is an outside "expert" (a man with a briefcase over fifty miles from home). When he says things like "close up the stockroom and make sure those inventory records are kept as close to perfection as is humanly possible," it will carry a lot more weight than it does when an insider tries to make the same points. He can sometimes be particularly effective with top management who almost always are being presented with many differing viewpoints and do not know just who is right and who is wrong. It is often said that the consultant usually goes around and finds out what people in the company think and then tells this to management. There is some truth to this. The tricky job for the consultant if figuring out which ideas are right and which are wrong. In almost any company there is a complete spectrum of opinions on almost any subject. So there is some value to having a consultant help you during this phase, but once again keep it to a minimum. Do as much of the job yourself as you possibly can.

This kind of education is challenging because a delicate balance must be struck. At first people are likely to throw up all the roadblocks they can ("Yeah, but what happens if there is a steel strike?"). This usually stems from the concepts of computer systems in comic book stories they have heard about — they are expecting something totally automatic and omnipotent.

The educators must restrain themselves from a reflex reaction at this point. They should *not,* in defending the new system, present it as a panacea. Systems are tools; they do not solve all the problems of a business. They merely provide better information so that people can use their time more effectively. The educators — especially the systems people who are caught up in their enthusiasm for the new system — *must resist the temptation to oversell!*

Management has a role to play here also. Many foremen, production control people, and other members of middle management are quick to reject a system that will not solve all of their problems. Too often they are looking for panaceas, and management must emphasize that there are none. The attitude frequently seems to be, "If we cannot solve all of the problems, why solve any?" Management needs to assume a realistic posture about systems and convey this throughout the organization.

They should also emphasize the need to keep the old system working while the new one is being installed. It is very tempting to assume that the new system will cure all ills and to stop exerting the effort required to keep the old informal system going.

CONVERSION — THE ODDS AND THE STAKES

There are three generally recognized methods for converting from an old system to a new system. They are

1. Try to run the old system and the new system in parallel.
2. Switch over to the new system "cold turkey."
3. Set up a "pilot" system.

The idea of running parallel operations is very appealing. Unfortunately it usually does not work for two principal reasons:

1. Very few companies have enough people available to run two systems effectively at the same time.
2. The users will always understand the old system better than they do the new system. It is very likely that *it* will survive and the new system will fail as a result.

The "cold turkey" approach has a great deal of appeal also.

On a given day the whole system is going to be converted over-night. This approach is extremely risky. People are not perfect. No complex system has ever been designed without having *some* flaws in it, and when the whole system is switched over at once there is a very, very great risk that the problems will be insurmountable. People's ability to contend with problems goes down as the square of the number of problems they have to work on. Double the problems, they have four times more trouble handling them. Triple them, they have nine times more trouble handling them. It is very easy for the problems to get out of control. Mass chaos will result. At this point the systems designer — who just knew he had thought of all possible contingencies — tries to work a 48-hour day straightening out the problems that have come up.

The proponents of the cold turkey approach claim that it is a great motivator, since people recognize that they have to sink or swim. In real life not many drownings have occurred through lack of motivation.

The pilot approach is the most distasteful approach, particu-larly to data processing people, but also the most practical. If, for example, a material requirements planning system is being put in, a particular product line should be isolated. The initial reaction everybody has when told this is that there is no product line that can be isolated. This is almost always pure baloney. Somehow, rather than install systems properly, people seem to prefer install-ing them improperly and then spend more effort firefighting and scrambling in trying to get it out of trouble. There is almost al-ways a way to set up the pilot system, if people are willing to go to the trouble.

Because pilot systems often involve duplicate files and double processing of transactions, they tend to be very unpopular with data processing people. They hasten to point out that the whole system might as well be switched over at once because the computer program must be completely written for a pilot system. From a programming point of view a pilot system requires as much, and often more, effort than the complete system.

This attitude begs the question, of course. The reasons in favor of the pilot system are not computer reasons, they are *people* reasons.

1. The pilot system is a way to keep the debugging problems to a manageable level.
2. The pilot system can often provide a way to determine whether or not the predicted results *can* really be achieved.
3. The pilot system is a way to train people without the chaos attendant to a cold turkey switch-over.
4. Running a pilot system in conjunction with the old system gives the users a chance to compare them realistically. No system will solve all of their problems; no system will work if people are not convinced that it is better. The pilot system is an effective sales tool.

Once the pilot has proved successful the new system can be installed in other areas rapidly. As long as the objectives of debugging, training, and selling have been met there is no further reason to delay in getting the system fully operative.

A pilot system is, of course, a vertical slice of the system. It is possible also to install horizontal slices to the system. For example, in the case of a material requirements planning system it would be possible to install the stock status report for all items before actually putting in the requirements plan. When the requirements plan was installed, it could be used for rescheduling initially before actually being used to order. This is not as practical or as useful as the pilot approach because it does not serve the training or selling objectives as effectively. It does serve to break the system down into manageable chunks, however, so that it can be installed and debugged without having a major debacle.

Some companies have used the cold turkey approach successfully. Some people have gone over Niagara Falls in a barrel successfully. When contemplating any gamble there are two things to be considered. The odds and the stakes. The odds that the system can be installed cold turkey may be very good indeed, but the stakes are extremely high. Many businesses have been ruined by computer systems that were installed by optimists.

The people who do the actual implementation should obviously be the users and not the systems people. A shop foreman explaining a new system to his superiors is always more credible than anyone who has the stigma of "computer" or "systems" attached to them.

KEEPING THE SHIP AFLOAT

Everyone who works with systems should have a motto hanging on his wall that says, "**Above all, do not make it worse.**" A system should be installed with great caution and without changing too many things. Consider the example used throughout this book, materials requirements planning. When installing this kind of system, the lot sizing techniques that you have been using in the past should not be changed very much. It may be necessary to modify them somewhat simply because the material requirements planning system is being installed, but if the planners have been ordering three-month lot sizes in the past, it is best to order three-month lot sizes when the system first goes in. Later on, the sizes can be changed. After the system is working, if the lot sizes are changed at the same time the material requirements planning system is installed, foremen may easily become critical of material requirements planning because of the greater number of set-ups that they have in the plant. It is just not worth taking this kind of risk.

Do not forget, also, to have fire drill procedures and perhaps even practices. People do not react well when the chips are down. Pre-plan what to do in case the computer does not work, or if parts of the system do not work. And have back-up procedures. These may simply be the manual methods used before the new system was installed. But you can be sure that if emergency procedures are not spelled out people will tend to panic. And you can also be sure that, at this moment in time, people who could tell them what to do are going to be fully occupied trying to get this system back on the air again. Another good reason for using the pilot approach.

At this point the virtues of the simple system are quite obvious. If people can be shown that the system is simple — if the logic is transparent — they will tend to support it. When a system is going through birth pains, sophistication can be a fatal liability.

At each step of the way there should be go/no-go checkpoints. Before the inventory system is put on the air, ensure that the records are accurate enough, that the bills of material are accurate enough. If they are not, stop. Avoid the snowball effect. It is so easy to get started with the system and then have too many excuses not to stop. This is not to say that this system should not be pushed forward with all possible effort. It is to say that every possible precaution needs to be taken to ensure that the system goes in successfully.

Above all, the systems installer should not burn his bridges. The informal systems kept the company running in the past. It is easy to predict that the new system will work because it is better. No one ever installed a system without great expectations. *But what if it does not work?*

In more than one company a not quite effective new system was installed, and the old informal system was destroyed simultaneously. One company installed a new — and very poorly designed — system for inventory control "cold turkey." They not only destroyed all manual records but also transferred many of the people who made the informal system work. Result: chaos.

Everyone who works on systems has a responsibility to his company to make sure that they avert the kind of disaster that has been all too common because of over-optimistic implementation. The best systems implementer is the "happy pessimist" who expects problems and tries to prepare for each of them while keeping the system implementation steps small and manageable. Once he has passed some of the check points, once he has the pilot system installed and working and the people trained, then he can "pull the big switch" and rapidly install much larger chunks of the system. Remembering the high stakes involved, he can take the pains to be sure to avert disaster, and he can stack the odds greatly in his favor that his system will go in successfully and produce results.

I, WE, YOU

The systems man is the instigator. He is the idea man who suggested to management some better ways of getting things done. Hopefully, management was trying to improve operating performance and came to him looking for help. At that point, he is in "I" mode. He is trying to sell ideas and to get people interested. Later he becomes part of the system development team. Not designing, but acting as the catalyst, trying to get the job done as "WE" work together on the project. More and more as the project progresses, he must fade into the background and transfer the responsibility for the system to the user. Severing the umbilical cord and getting into "YOU" mode is sometimes one of the most difficult systems problems. But it must be done. During the installation of the pilot, for example, he can nurse the system along, but at that point he should turn to the users and ask if *they* are ready to go ahead, if *they* believe they can get the results they said they could, and if *they* are willing to take the next steps to install a successful operations-oriented system.

7

*Using Systems
to Manage*

"Systems are necessary, but not sufficient."

FIREFIGHTING WAS FUN

It is ironic that, since computer systems are now responsive enough so that the formal system can generate control information, many companies find the last hurdle to be the biggest. People do not seem to like being systematic. The most universal human drive is a seeking for significance, and firefighting is a heroic role.

Consider the foreman, for example, who is told that every stockroom transaction must be properly recorded or the inventory system will not work. He has been given accolades by his boss in the past for getting the shipments out at the end of the month "by hook or by crook," even when that meant stealing parts from the stockroom. Now he is being told that if *he* will be sure that his people handle paperwork properly the system will do a better job of getting him the parts he needs.

If management is going to get successful systems installed they need to measure people on their contributions to a team effort. Every hero who prides himself on firefighting is usually among the greatest causes of the problems he gets so much glory for "solving."

This was natural in the days when formal systems could not possibly generate information that was up-to-date enough to control. The hero was the man who could get things done in spite of the system.

And the informal system usually functions in a way that shows him that he is really doing his job but others are not! Consider these examples:

1. The assembly foreman takes parts from the stockroom without making out the proper paperwork. This, of course, generates incorrect inventory records; when these cause shortages at a later date he finds it difficult to understand why the people in inventory control — or perhaps the computer — "always get loused up."

2. A formal inventory system that is not capable of maintaining the proper priorities on parts will almost always show many items to be late when they are not really needed (because their priorities have changed and the system did not recognize it). Parts that the formal system did not order soon enough usually *do* get ordered or expedited by the informal system. Selective interpretation of this information gives the inventory control man a feeling that he is performing yeoman service against staggering odds. He observes that frequently when he *does* need a part it was long overdue. (He does not notice that almost all open purchase and shop orders are late and that he really needs very few of them.) He complains that if purchasing and the factory only did the work on schedule he

would have no problems (he probably would have no job also since there would not be any place to store all the late material if it suddenly did come in on schedule).

Frequently none of these people realize that the informal system is obsolete — that they need a formal system that will help them out of their endless firefighting. And it requires a real selling job to convince them that the problems are *theirs,* that *they* need to make the formal systems work, not the systems people.

They are often skeptical about "systems" from past experience. They have been razzle-dazzled by the computer types before. People who, in their exuberance, oversold systems that probably were more notable for their sophistication than their soundness. Having survived these past efforts without seeing any real changes has merely reinforced the operating man's skepticism about systems.

Even though they have lived through Phases 1, 2, and 3 (see Chapter 1, Phase 1 — informal systems controls, Phase 2 — drifting out of control, Phase 3 — out of control), they often fail to see that the informal system is no longer capable of controlling.

A business increase will make them slide from Phase 1 to Phase 2. The symptoms of Phase 2 are reliable:

Everyone works harder and harder while the situation gets worse and worse.

Often about this time the "quick fixes" get trotted out, and these only serve to move the company into Phase 3 faster! Consider the case of Harry.

Harry was an old shop man. He had once been a toolmaker, then a foreman, then plant superintendent, and was now plant manager. One day he asked to have his inventory system reviewed since there were occasional reports of parts shortages at the assembly line.

A review showed that the inventory records were inaccurate.

Inventory planners would check component availability before sending an assembly order down to the stockroom to have the components pulled and sent into the assembly department. If all the components for a particular order were supposed to be on hand, they would send the assembly order down to the stockroom. Inevitably, because their inventory records were inaccurate, one or two of the components that were supposed to be on hand were not. This caused the occasional shortages on the assembly line that Harry had noted.

Harry was told that this system lacked integrity. That the inventory records could not be believed, and that it would be a good idea to lock up the stockroom and develop procedures for handling paperwork within the stockroom, train the stockpickers, set objectives for the stockroom manager in keeping records accurately rather than just getting material out to the floor as fast as he could, and, in general, developing a program for improving the integrity of the system. This amused Harry no end. "System integrity" sounded like one more buzz word. His reaction was swift and disasterous. Since inventory records were inaccurate, he authorized a complete inventory of the stockroom on Saturday. It is difficult enough to take a well-planned physical inventory once a year with trained people; impromptu inventories on a crash basis almost always generate more incorrect inventory figures than there were to start with. This is exactly what happened to Harry.

With more incorrect figures the situation got worse. Harry still refused to take the problem of system integrity seriously. He decided that the best way to handle the problem would be to take all of the assembly orders from the next month and pull all of the material needed for them. He would then find out what the shortages were and make sure his expediters got that material through the shop. Pulling this much material from the stockroom required a great deal of overtime and pretty soon the aisles were jammed with partial assembly orders. "Partial" because with each order that was pulled there were fewer parts left in inventory, so that almost every order went out incomplete at this point. In fact, since there were many common components, part A, which might be the only part missing from one assembly order, would not be available in the component storeroom because it had already been pulled and was sitting on a skid waiting for another assembly order that was missing part B. Having created his own artificial shortages through his second attempt at a crash program, Harry watched his performance in the assembly department go from bad to worse.

Harry's story is all too common. There are a great many managers today who are not ready to face up to the problems of managing with a system. They thrive on the firefighting and living from crisis to crisis. They have seen the company go through Phase 3 (symptoms: **Everyone blames everyone else and the president often winds up answering the customers' phoned-in complaints).** [1]

But each time the company recovers — usually because the situation has become stable enough for the informal system to take control (temporarily!) — they congratulate themselves on having solved the problems! Like a man who has been shoveling snow all winter, they look up in the spring and say, "We did it! It's gone. Thank God that cannot happen again!"

But it can. The engineers, salesmen, and customers are creating more new products. More experienced people are retiring. Next winter is sure to come. And it will be tougher than the last one. But people do not seem to recognize this when they are back in Phase 1. They often feel complacent and overconfident, not realizing that their informal system only works when everything is just right.

Most companies today need formal systems to help them control. Each pendulum swing into Phase 3 tends to be a little

---

[1] While writing this, I read the following description of the death throes of one of the brokerage houses that went defunct in the 1970 recession. An article titled "House of Cards", *The Wall Street Journal*, December 11, 1970, stated:

> "The consultants also 'noted evidence of a general lack of cooperation and communication between various departments of the operations division.' They said, 'Symptoms of the problem were noted in the excessive criticism of one department by another, as well as the tendency to (transfer) a problem from one department to another, instead of finding a solution and correcting the problem."

Obviously, the advanced stages of Phase 3.

worse and more nerve wracking. More than one coronary has resulted from the sheer frustration of trying to run a business with an informal system that simply cannot control anymore.

Management has a job to do to get a realistic, responsible attitude toward systems by the users. No amount of effort in the programming department can make a system work if the users do not see the need and accept their responsibility for getting results.

There is a real problem here in that many of the middle managers today do not see the need for systems. They are too close to the problem even to recognize it, and, in fact, they tend to view systems as the province of the beard and sneaker set who fool around with things like computers. Too often when new systems are being developed they are aloof and detached. Wondering "if those systems guys will pull it off this time. . . ."

But, of course, much of the reason for their attitude is that they have not had it explained to them. Most foremen can understand that they are using an inefficient informal system — they see the expedite lists! Most of them can remember having been in Phase 3 at some time. And the last thing they want is more of *that*. If the system can be presented as a way out of Phase 3 — a way to get a system that will help them to do their jobs with less chaos and more results — most of them will respond. But they need to see systems as bread and butter tools for them and not as wild-blue-yonder ideas from the systems boys.

THE GAME OF MANAGEMENT — ANYONE CAN PLAY

There are many aspects of management, but three areas are most important. These three were picked because their absence in a number of companies has kept these companies from ever being able to do anything very substantial in improving their performance.

1. **Failure to set proper objectives.** This term "management by objectives" has become a cliche today and many com-

panies have said, "We tried it and it did not work for us." But management by objectives never does work by itself. It is just a way of making sure that people understand what they are supposed to do so that they will work toward the *proper* overall company objectives. Just sitting down and thinking about these objectives can straighten out an awful lot of the fundamental problems. Take the example of the purchasing agent who is more concerned with getting parts in at the lowest possible cost than getting parts in on time to keep the assembly line running. People have suggested many changes in organization to cure this problem, but, inevitably, when the problem exists it is because the only real objective that he is working to is bringing parts in at the lowest cost. He is probably measured quite rigorously against this objective while nobody has given him the overall objective of getting the parts in on time, nor do they have any effective way of measuring his performance against this objective (and it may very well be that the inventory system is so poor that it does not provide reasonable, truthful priorities against which his performance can be measured).

Management by objectives should, of course, be concerned not just with the day-to-day objectives that the man is supposed to meet on a routine basis, but also with a few significant improvements that he is supposed to make during the year. These should be only those few of vital importance to the company in executing its "game plan."

2. **Failure to develop people.** Business has done a good job of keeping the personnel recruiting agencies in business. Always looking for the good people on the outside. Townsend said it very well:[2]

"Probably whenever Sitting Bull, Geronimo, and the other chiefs pow-wowed, the first topic of conversation was the shortage of Indians. Certainly today no meeting of the high-and-mighty is complete

---

[2] Robert Townsend, *Up the Organization*, New York, N.Y.: Alfred A. Knopf, Inc., 1970.

until someone polishes the conventional wisdom: 'Our big trouble today is getting enough good people.' This is crystal clear nonsense."

The responsibility of management is developing people. Most managers are so busy doing today's job that they forget about developing people for tomorrow and the results are plain to see.

In fact, this is exactly the message that we get from *The Peter Principle*.[3] Peter, of course, pointed out that in any organization people tend to get promoted until they rise to their level of incompetence. This is humorous because it is often true. Peter goes on to use the example of the toolmaker who is promoted to foreman. The company now has a poor foreman and has lost a good toolmaker. This too is true — but why? *Primarily because management never took the time to train this man to be a good foreman.* He probably still thinks it his most important job to make tools, when, in fact, his most important job is providing leadership for other people.

The Peter principle assumes that people fall neatly onto a scale of competence or incompetence. The fact of the matter is that practically everybody falls somewhere in between the two extremes. There *are* a few people who are so competent that they can move into any job and perceive what the objectives are and start managing well. There are also a few people who are so incompetent that no matter how much guidance they were given, they would not be able to handle the job. Most people, however, when properly directed, shown what the objectives are, and given the kind of management attention needed can do a good job.

The Peter principle tells us that we have failed miserably at management. The only people who are successful today are those few who are extremely competent or those few who have been lucky enough to work for man-

---

[3] Laurence F. Peter and Raymond Hill, *The Peter Principle*, New York, N.Y.: William Morrow and Co., Inc., 1969.

agers who *did* take the time to give them the guidance they needed. There is evidence everywhere that we are squandering our most important resource — people — through lack of good management. Every manager should be taught, retaught, and taught again that the main job of management is growing people.

3. **Developing teamwork.** In Chapter 1, we discussed a company in which teamwork was poor and life was one continuous round of "who shot John." The president of this company spent most of his time refereeing. Deciding who was "right" and who was "wrong." What a waste of time. Every time he figured out who was right, the person who was wrong figured out how not to get caught again. The result is what Parkinson described as "injelititis."[4] Injelititis is a combination of incompetence and jealousy, where everybody in the organization spends their time defending their position and competing as strongly as they can against each other.

Teamwork is a hackneyed word, yet it is one of the major areas of management failure. We have something to learn here from the typical dictator. Nasser was one of the most popular rulers of Egypt. Whether or not he truly accomplished a great deal is irrelevant here, his people loved him and for a very good reason. Whenever the chips were down he pointed to Israel and said "Look out for them!"

Every dictator learns this strategy. Make the people worry about the enemy outside and they will stop squabbling among themselves and start pulling together. No country is as dedicated to its purpose as a company fighting a war for its very survival. At this point almost everybody competes against the enemy outside rather than against each other.

And we can learn something here about business. In fact,

---

[4] C. Northcote Parkinson, *Parkinson's Law*, Boston, Mass.: Houghton-Mifflin Company, 1962, page 78.

Townsend learned it but evidently did not know that he had. He certainly failed to make the point in his book. When his advertising agency came up with the motto "We are only number two, but we try harder" this automatically told everyone who number one was and who the real competition was! A *great* way to generate teamwork!

People love to compete. They play golf, they play cards, and they wager, yet businessmen have been relatively unsuccessful in harnessing the urge for competition constructively. When it is not directed properly the result is injelititis. When it is harnessed properly, by telling people right down at the machine operator level who the competition is, how the company is doing, why that new product is needed, and how we are doing against our goals, significant strides forward can be made. Teamwork *is* a hackneyed word. All the important things have been said before. It just does not seem like anybody was listening the first few hundred times.

Today we hear much discussion about management "style," and some managers certainly do have some rather bizarre approaches to leading people. Some do not lead at all, they simply act as caretakers. Others constantly foment crisis — one company has switched one product back and forth between two plants four times in three years — and it never seems to occur to them that the quality control problems that haunt them exist largely because neither plant has ever made the product long enough to learn how!

Consider the example of the company that had a problem with parts. Some of them were used in production and also for service. The service department insisted that when a part was in short supply *they* should receive it because they needed to keep customer's machines running. On the other hand, the assembly department claimed they should have highest priority because without the part they could not meet their shipping goals. The first solution to this problem that was tried was to set up a separate service parts inventory in another part of the factory. But that did not seem to do much. When the assembly foreman wanted parts he simply took them from the service parts storeroom. On the other hand when the service parts people *really* had a machine breakdown in the field and lacked the part they would take the part from the assembly storeroom! Management had not solved the problem, but they had increased their inventory and their storeroom costs because they were now keeping the same part in two locations. The next solution proposed for this problem was to build a separate service parts warehouse in a town ten miles away. After the warehouse was built, the company had to invest in trucks that were kept running constantly back and forth between the assembly storeroom and the service parts warehouse!

The problem here was a very fundamental one. Inventory is a limited resource. Someone needs to be given the responsibility of deciding how it is going to be used when it is in short supply. Management needs to teach people how to make decisions when the only ones open are bad ones. How to pick the "least worst" choice.

Today management is an amateur's game. Anyone can play, anyone can use his own style. Watch professional golfers and you will see some variations in style, but most of them have learned a basic set of principles. We have not done a very good job of sorting out and identifying the basic principles of business management. If anything, the interest in systems, computers, and techniques such as PERT, exponential smoothing, linear programming, Management Information Systems, and the like have distracted us from the main business of business — managing people and teaching them what business is *really* all about.

THE MOMENT OF TRUTH

Now that the new system is on the air, management needs to insist on operational results. When the pilot program was run, they should have seen some of these results before approving and going ahead with the balance of the system. Regular performance measures should be maintained to see that the people are able to use the new tools to get results. If the six keys to systems success have been followed religiously, the system should produce results. Those keys are restated in the final section of the book, *Checklists for the Executive.*

If the system did not work out successfully, many symptoms can be identified, but the six keys will tell you where the real diseases are. Probably the biggest problem of all in getting systems to be successful, and the most likely place for the system to fall down, is in getting the user to assume the responsibility for some systems success. Frequently, people will take a man out of the user group, have him work with the systems people, but then, when the system is installed, they find that the man who has the responsibility for getting results was not involved enough to feel that the system is his. The former user who moves into the systems group is now identified as a systems man. Every step of the way, make sure that the man who is going to manage the system is assuming the responsibility for systems success and will not use the system as an excuse. This is a very, very difficult problem to put to bed. Every time you think you have, take a look behind you because you will probably find that it needs to be attended to one more time.

Some of the symptoms for systems failure are pretty common, and people will be quick to identify them. One of the most common complaints of the systems people is that management did not *make* people follow the system. This betrays a very simplistic view of management. Many people think that management only consists of giving orders. Actually there is little hope of disciplining people to use something that does not make sense to them. If the users do not want to make the system work or do not want to follow it, the chances are that one of the six keys, or perhaps many of them, was ignored.

Another symptom that can be somewhat misleading is the complaint that the information in the system is inaccurate, and if people would only handle the information properly everything would be fine. Some integrity can be designed into a system, but integrity will only be maintained if people understand the system and *depend* upon it. Only then will they take the trouble to keep it accurate. A system that is not sound, for example, will not be maintained properly. The typical inventory control system in most companies today cannot truly control priorities, and an informal system has to do it. As a result, very few companies can boast accurate inventory records since people do not really depend upon them.

The manager should also have the system audited periodically to be sure that it is working properly. It is very easy for the informal system to start creeping back in again. In the case of a material requirements plan, for example, this is fairly easy to identify. Are people working on parts based on the priorities the formal system generates, or is there only a facade of a formal system, with handwritten expedite lists really controlling the priorities?

If the system does not really work, *do something*. Most companies just continue to limp along, paying for the computer, paying for the system, and not getting the results. They should either get a system that will work or get rid of the computer and have the payroll done down at the local bank. Too few managers have had guts enough to face up to this basic issue.

SYSTEM CONTINUITY — A HAUNTING PROBLEM

No system is any better than the man who uses it, and the poor workman always tends to blame his tools. Most companies today have poor systems, but as they get better systems there will *still* be pressure to change. Beyond that, anyone who has worked on systems knows how easy it is for them to fall into disrepair and disuse. Systems continuity is a spectre that haunts the experienced systems man. Dr. Joseph Orlicky asked:

> "Will the business manager of the future be able to learn enough about the internal logic of a complex system? This is an intriguing question to which there is no satisfactory answer known at present. It can serve as food for thought about how to deal with a management problem that

now only looms on the horizon, and for which special solution techniques may yet have to be invented."[5]

There is no one simple black and white solution to this problem, but there are a number of things that can be done:

1. Managers should be impressed with their responsibility as stewards. They have their area of the business in trust to run, certainly, but they must pass it on to the next generation of managers. One of the objectives that should be set for each manager is to maintain, continue, and, *only if necessary,* revise systems he is responsible for in his own department.

2. The problem of systems continuity presents one of the most convincing arguments of all for avoiding over-sophistication. Simple systems tend to be easy to understand and they tend to survive. Sophisticated systems very seldom outlast their designer's tenure. They are too readily identified with one man, and when he goes the system usually dies.

3. The more successfully companies can use standard approaches to their problems, the more successful they will be in keeping the systems operating successfully. The company that uses a standard approach to material requirements planning rather than inventing its own will find that as new people move into the company they are more likely to be familiar with the system rather than veiwing it as something strange, foreign, and not particularly useful to them. Standardization runs against the very grain of many systems men who pride themselves on their creativity, but the use of standard programs offers the greatest hope there is for putting in systems that will not get thrown out every two years.

4. The last chapter covered the subject of procedures and the importance of writing procedures that express the sys-

---

[5] *The Successful Computer System,* New York, N.Y.: McGraw-Hill Book Co., 1969, page 174.

tem's intent and objectives. It is just as important to indicate in these procedures some of the things that can be done to destroy the system, and to issue cautions against them. One company, for example, with an excellent materials requirements planning system on a computer, had their inventory increase and their delivery performance drop off very, very badly when somebody came up with a bright idea of adding a little more "safety time to each item." The high-value components were ordered with due dates a week before they were really needed. The medium-value components had due dates two weeks before they were needed, and the low-value components four weeks before they were needed. In spite of their ability to replan requirements, the dates that were put on the component orders were no longer valid. A foreman could easily be working on a low-value item that had an order due date showing that it was needed in the current week, when in fact, he should have been working on a high-value item that had an order due date showing that it was needed next week. This confused the issue completely and in a very short period of time, hand-written expedite lists became the real system and performance deteriorated dramatically.

Specific cautions about this subtle type of abuse of the system should be included in the prologue to the procedure. It should be explained that the purpose of the material requirements planning system is to establish and maintain proper priorities on component parts orders. Examples should be given like that above to indicate how the validity of priorities can be destroyed in various ways. The systems designers will not be able to imagine all of the ways to abuse the system, but if they explain its intent properly and provide a few examples, hopefully, intelligent managers will be able to understand what must be done to keep the system from degenerating.

5. The system should be audited periodically, and here is another place where the systems designer can perform a very valuable function indeed. If he really understands

how the system works, he should be able to point out some key indicators so that management can really know whether the system is working properly. In a materials requirements planning system, for example, the number of late orders in the shop is a partial indication of the validity of the requirements plan. If the master schedule is being overstated, this can generate a great number of late orders. The "in-stock" dates on components that are being expedited because they were not available when the assembly order was issued can also be a very good indicator. If these dates tend to fall at random, the system is not functioning properly. The dates should show that these items were due to be in stock when the assembly order was issued.

These are merely presented as examples of the types of key indicators that should be audited periodically to make sure the system is functioning properly.

6. There should be a procedure — just like the procedure for making engineering changes in a manufacturing company — that is used to make changes to the system. Most engineering changes have to be approved by marketing, engineering, manufacturing, and financial people. The same type of formal change procedure should be required for systems changes once the system has been installed.

There are no easy answers to the problems of system continuity and probably every system is bound to be replaced someday, but each manager is responsible both for keeping systems expense to a minimum and for keeping people's attention focused on the important job of managing the business with the system, rather than constantly redesigning and tinkering with it.

A FOND FAREWELL TO THE AGE OF ALCHEMY

Those marvelous men and their magic machines convinced us — and themselves — that they were going to revolutionize the business world with Operations Research, Management Science, and Management Information Systems. Practically none of this has come to pass. Instead we have found that the big payoff applications for the computer have been in the massive manipulation of data. The much touted techniques of scientific inventory management, for example, have had very little success, primarily because there are not too many real payoff applications. The technique of material requirements planning, which is very mundane, has paid off, and paid off handsomely. The computer can keep the priorities on all parts up to date and enable us to replace the informal system with a formal system.

We have seen this in many other areas, forecasting for one. Many esoteric mathematical techniques for forecasting have been developed. Very few of them have really been successful, but the computer has helped us substantially by being able to store, retrieve, and analyze data by using very simple rules. Better forecasts can now be made. The routine forecasts are made by the computer using such techniques as moving averages, and the others are made by people using the power of the computer to make the data available to them in useful form.

This does not mean that there is not some application for some of the more mathematical approaches. Linear programming has been used in a few instances to help companies operate more profitably. But it is not this type of analysis program that really holds the payoff for most companies. It is the bread and butter operational control system that can really help *people* to produce results.

At some vantage point in the future we will look back upon the early years of computer application and see them in their true perspective. The early years were the years of alchemy. Consider this quote from *The World Book Encyclopedia:*[6]

Alchemy was a mixture of science and magic practiced in ancient

---

[6] *The World Book Encyclopedia*, Volume 1, 1962, page 278.

times. . . . One of the main purposes of alchemy was to change less costly metals into gold and silver. Another was to find a substance, called the elixir of life, that would cure all ailments. Alchemists failed to achieve either purpose, but they made valuable chemical discoveries.

We look back in wonderment at the practice of alchemy. These men never did do what they set out to do. Yet they kept trying, and trying, and trying. They kept reassuring each other that it really was going to happen someday. They kept telling the people they worked for that with a little more patience, and a little more investment, they really could transmute base metal into gold. Amazing, isn't it, that alchemy flourished for several hundred years before we realized that the real value was in chemistry. Perhaps in the field of business we will be able to accelerate that transition and to recognize both the folly of oversophisticated wizardry and the necessity for practical formal systems.

The four checklists that follow are an attempt to distill out some of the key points in this book. They should be useful to the executive for future reference.

Checklists for

The Executive

checklist one

Six Keys to Systems Success

1. Do not make the system too sophisticated. The major payoff applications today fall into the category of "massive manipulation of data" rather than mathematical optimization. Insist that people use a "value analysis" approach and leave out the frills. Sophistication[1] is the greatest single cause of user distrust of systems.

2. Make sure the application is sound. (See Checklist Four.)

3. Be sure that the users develop their *own* systems with the help of systems people. Above all, *be sure that the users*

---

[1] *Sophisticated:* "Deprived of its native simplicity; intellectually appealing." Merriam-Webster Dictionary, 1963.

have assumed the responsibility for the success of the system.

4. Be sure that the system is designed to help people to do their jobs, rather than with the naive idea that the system is going to control the business.

5. Use a pilot program to implement. Do it very, very cautiously and be very careful not to destroy the informal system until you are sure that the formal system works.

6. Do the homework where it really counts. Be sure that paperwork transactions are going to be handled properly. Be sure that basic documents such as bills of material are correct. Be sure that proper part numbers are maintained — the computer requires *unique identifiers*. Be sure that the people who handle the paperwork understand why it must be observed religiously if the formal system is to work for them.

checklist two

Systems Shibboleths

Just as sailors in the days of Columbus interpreted their observations incorrectly and believed that the earth was flat, the people involved in systems work have often grossly misinterpreted their experiences. The following shibboleths are among the most widely held.

1. "If the systems people do not take the initiative there won't be any new systems."

It is a sad commentary on management's attitude toward systems that systems people are usually the instigators who are trying to sell the users on better systems, rather than the users coming begging for systems help because management has insisted on better performance and the users see systems as a means to that end.

Nevertheless, the systems man cannot *assume the responsibility for systems success and must, in spite of his frustrations,* not *take the initiative away from the user.*

2. "The system failed because management did not enforce discipline."

Many people with little line management experience have a simplistic view of management as a simple hierarchy of authority where orders are given to subordinates at each level. In fact, especially in the United States today, the actual business world is far different. The prohibition law could not be enforced because it did not have popular support; laws on murder generally can be enforced because most people believe in them. In an organization, the need for a system must be sold *to the users. Only when there is a "critical mass" of believers can the discipline be enforced.*

3. "Our management does not understand; they are not sophisticated."

Most line management people do not recognize the need to use systems and they do not take a realistic attitude toward systems. Management must *learn to use systems to manage. But systems people can help by de-emphasizing "sophistication" — the greatest barrier to a realistic user attitude toward systems — and by making sure they are selling, but not overselling, management on the practical operating advantages of computer based systems.*

4. "We can build that right into the system — the computer can easily handle that logic."

Virtually no information systems are good enough to produce results if people won't use them intelligently. When people do not understand systems they will either follow them blindly or ignore them completely. The question is not whether the computer can handle the logic but rather whether adding this "decision making" function to the computer logic will jeopardize system transparency.

5. "We have to develop our own systems because

(a) our problems are unique,

(b) canned programs are not efficient, and

(c) we do not want to get locked into some vendor's software."

Standard application programs must be examined carefully. Some are excellent — some are extremely naive and just could not work (remember that the supplier does not assume any responsibility for the soundness of the application!). But standard application programs are useful and should be used whenever possible because:

(a) *Most companies' problems are not unique. They only look that way to the unprofessional people who see their own problems in a parochial light. Users are often guilty of this posture. Systems people accept it too readily because it gives them an excuse to re-invent the wheel and this is a basic lust in the heart of most "designers."*

(b) *Packaged software is often not very efficient from a technical point of view. But the speed of installation, greater assurance of application soundness, better documentation, and other operational considerations are far more important than computer run time.*

(c) *The greatest advantage of standard approaches is the greater potential for systems continuity. Too many "home-brewed" systems become "personality dependent" and never function well after the systems designer has quit, been promoted, etc. Better to be locked into a vendor's software than your systems/ DP man's software.*

checklist three

Management Shibboleths

1. "Why bother with better systems — we are making money."

The seeds of disaster are usually sown when things are going well. To be sure, systems should not be developed for the sake of having systems, but few companies can compete successfully in today's complex business world for very long without good formal systems. And very few companies have them! Many companies are successful today only because their competition is no better than they are.

2. "Management people are too busy running the company to fool around with the systems."

Systems are tools for managers to use to run the business better. If they do not appreciate them as means to that end they are naive. The managers must break through the "sophistication" barrier and see systems in a mature business perspective. The responsibility for systems cannot be delegated to technicians.

3. "Our computer systems have not paid off so we are going to hire an expert computer systems man."

Systems failures are as much a responsibility of management people as systems people. If management had supported systems efforts and insisted that the six systems keys (checklist number one) be followed they probably wouldn't have to replace their present computer systems man!

4. "We are hiring a consultant to design and install our computer system."

Fantastic! This is too often an easy way to duck responsibility. It is expensive — but it is only the stockholders' money! In this day of technological acceleration consultants can perform a useful function. But management should view them as catalysts and not reactors. The responsibility for systems success cannot be delegated to consultants.

5. "That theory about locking the stockrooms to ensure accurate inventory records is great, but it is not practical in our company."

Management personnel who gained their experience when there was no practical way to have formal systems that controlled are often the greatest cause of systems failure. When the cost reduction season comes, for example, they eliminate the people who were maintaining basic systems information, like manufacturing bills of material. Until management takes a mature attitude toward systems the investment is a waste of money at least. At worst this attitude is an irresponsible squandering of the company's potential for competing in the current — and future — business environment.

checklist four

Determining Payoff Applications, Some Questions and Answers

1. *Where are the problems that better information could help to solve?* Remember that computers are tools that have proved most successful in manipulating massive amounts of data. What are your problems? How could better information help solve them?

2. *Are my systems people — and even more important, the users — up to date on computer applications?* Usually the systems people are better informed than the users on modern applications; while both groups usually still have plenty to learn, management should do everything possible to get these groups to communicate better. The systems man often assumes a posture of superiority and

167

sophistication that alienates the user. The user is often "too busy drowning to save himself."

3. *Where can we get up-to-date application education?* Courses taught by the American Management Association and consulting firms and computer manufacturers are available. University sponsored continuing education programs and in-plant training programs[1] can also be of value. But, before spending money and wasting time, investigate them. Get references from past attendees. Price is not an indication of quality nor is it an important consideration. Insist on the *best* available. Your systems people are often well-informed on this type of education and can investigate and recommend good sources.

4. *Can the computer salesman help in determining payoff applications?* He certainly can. A good one is well-informed about what other companies are doing and can draw on application expertise within his own company. Of course, he only gets paid if he sells something, so his advice should be weighed carefully. He can, however, be an excellent source for references so that you can see other companies using an application before trying it yourself.

5. *What about the consultant?* A good one should be able to help you identify payoff applications and give you references to other companies where you can see the application successfully working. Remember, however, that, while the consultant often speaks disdainfully of the computer salesman, he frequently has had less company-sponsored education and thus may not be as competent to recommend sound applications. And, of course, he frequently is on the same type of incentive bonus program as the computer salesman, only he is in the business of renting bodies instead of hardware.

---

[1] One of the newer techniques that has proved effective is video-assisted instruction. The user company typically buys an inexpensive video tape player for in-plant training. Professionally developed courses can then be taught to small groups at their own pace, providing a continuing source of in-house education.

Index

A

B

T